WORLDVIEW SKILLS

Transforming conflict from the inside out

JESSIE SUTHERLAND

Foreword by Chief Robert Joseph

WORLDVIEW STRATEGIES

Book Cover Design: Hilary Percy and Blair Cummock
Seaspiral photo courtesy of Paul Doherty
Printed by Blitzprint Inc.

ISBN 0-9736988-2-9

WORLDVIEW SKILLS

Transforming conflict from the inside out

To my family and friends with gratitude;

To Galiano Island whose beauty first opened my eyes
to the wondrous world;

To the whole world for being such a good teacher.

CONTENTS

FOREWORD

The world has much to learn about reconciliation between Indigenous people and their colonizers – the oppressed and their oppressors so to speak. Jessie Sutherland's book, *Worldview Skills: Transforming Conflicts From The Inside Out* may well be the insight that provides the greatest potential for bringing about the needed healing and reconciliation that must take place. It has the potential to provide the spark required to bring real peace, balance, and harmony between parties, between Canada and its Aboriginal people. I agree absolutely with Ms Sutherland's assertion that at the heart of reconciliation is essentially a parallel process of personal and political transformation from systems of dominance to relationships of mutuality.

The power and persuasion of healing and reconciliation is an unavoidable transformative process. It can and does happen one heart at a time and manifests politically as well, when mutual respect prevails.

The heart and soul, spirit and will of Canada's Aboriginal peoples was gutted for a long, long time. Thank God for their resilience.

There now is a contemporary process of reclamation and re-empowerment in the Aboriginal community. There is an affirmation of their genesis and history. They are reclaiming their languages and cultures as well as their own institutions of power. They are reasserting their rich and bountiful inheritance.

If ever there was an opportunity of mutuality and respectful worldviews the time can be no better than now. Canada should learn from its mistakes. The churches should learn from their mistakes. Jessie Sutherland's timely idea and book should help the parties in learning strategies in bringing about reconciliation.

Drawing on and using the four fundamental touchstones suggested by Ms. Sutherland, including worldviewing skills, is a must as Aboriginal people are once again standing on solid ground based on their worldviews.

I have always understood the devastating impact of worldview dominance by others. I have sensed the way back would be a mutual acceptance of such matters. Ms. Sutherland's book affirms this in the strongest way. Heart by heart, family by family, community by community is the most appealing way to bring about reconciliation and this I have learned from Ms. Sutherland.

Chief Robert Joseph

Hereditary Chief of the Gwa wa enuk First Nation

Chairman of Native American Leadership Alliance For Peace and Reconciliation

Special Advisor to Federal Government for Residential Schools

Former Executive Director of Indian Residential School Survivors Society of BC

Working Caucus on Residential Schools (Federal government, Churches, and Aboriginal parties working together)

Current Chairman of the Adjudicator Reference Group for ADR process

Working Caucus on Residential School for the Assembly of First Nations

PREFACE AND GRATITUDE

Throughout the world, many people yearn to transform relationships caught in deep-rooted conflict and cycles of violence. Some call for justice, others plead for peace at any cost. Most crave a different world, but either they don't know where to begin or they have become cynical that nothing ever works anyhow. *Worldview Skills: Transforming Conflicts From The Inside Out* offers a practical way to transform systems of domination into relationships of mutuality. This book grew out of Graduate research at the University of Victoria, which took me to various international peace institutes around the world. Moreover, it is the culmination of my own life's work and experience which has taken me to the Middle East; Europe; North, East, and West Africa; South America; and across Canada, including various northern Indigenous communities.

This book was written with two goals in mind. First, I hoped to provide a new framework about what genuine reconciliation entails. My intention was to develop new insights into the nature of deep-rooted conflict and how to create conditions for genuine reconciliation. Second, my hope was to provide practical and accessible skills and tools for everyone interested in working towards reconciliation in their own context.

With these aims in mind, I laid a theoretical and scholarly foundation and simultaneously wove stories and anecdotes throughout as a way to illustrate concrete skills and tools anyone can learn. This book should be read in consecutive order – each chapter builds on the knowledge and skills of the previous one.

In Part One, *The Way In*, I synthesize reconciliation and peace-building literature and offer a new framework for reconciliation. Part Two, *Worldviewing Skills*, uses storytelling as a way to tease out various skills for creating conditions for reconciliation. In Part Three, *The Way Out*, I conclude with details of the personal work necessary for transforming relationships and creating conditions for the genesis of a new era. For those interested in the "story behind the story," Appendix I describes the methodology and self-reflective research praxis I used in writing this book. While my hope is that this book in its entirety will be useful and readable to all; if you prefer to skip more academic writing (methodology and chapter one) the remainder of the book is self-contained.

I wish to extend appreciation and gratitude to all my family, friends, and colleagues from all corners of the Earth who have generously encouraged me throughout the research and writing of this book. Their support, insights, and friendship were invaluable in contributing to the final text.

This book began as graduate work at the University of Victoria and has since gone through various changes making it more accessible and for a wider audience. A warm thank you for the final push to completion to Hilary Percy for her graphic design and technical expertise; to Kathryn Rockwell for her thorough editing before going to press; to Suzanne Plourde for sharing her stories; and to Catherine Manekar for her generosity with her time and skills.

The following companies were also instrumental in the completion of this book: Ink Tree, Co-Creative Coaches, Wester Press, and Blitzprint.

I would also like to thank the many professors and advisors who assisted me during the research and writing of Masters thesis as much of this book is built on the work I did during that time: Dr. Frank Cassidy, Dr. Taiaiake Alfred, and Dr. Pat MacKenzie, Catherine Morris, Dr. James Tully, Dr.

Antoinette Oberg, Dr. Ben Hoffman, Maureen Maloney, Dr. Roger Hutchinson, Dr. Matt James, Michelle LeBaron, Dr. Hizkias Assefa, Dr. John Paul Lederach, Dr. Jayne Docherty, Dr. Barry Hart, Sam Doe, Dr. Chris Cuneen, Ray Peters, Dr. Peter Seixas, Dr. John Torpey, Ellen White and Leah Whiu.

I would like to extend my sincere thanks to the many people who read various parts or full drafts of my graduate thesis and whose feedback has been incorporated into this book: Dr. Ihab Banabila, Dorothy Christian, Ardyth Cooper, Harley Eagle, Lois Gardner, Chief Robert Joseph, Dr. Felix Kaputo, Perry Mbibong, Dr. Neil Sutherland, and Cathy Stubington.

A warm thank you to the many practitioners that shared freely their knowledge, experience, and resources: Al Fuertes, Bishop John Hanen, Maggie Hodgson, Yoshie Ikema, Yvonne Rigsby-Jones, Alex Nelson, Anne Nguyen, Bishop Ochola, Herbert O'Driscoll, Carrie Reid, Mary Alice Smith, Laura Stovel, Robert Vachon, Meneno Vamuzo, and Sister Audrey for sharing their knowledge and resources.

Many organizations and institutions made it possible to attend various international peace institutes and academic programs. A sincere thanks to the University of Victoria, Initiatives of Change, the Liu Centre for Global Studies (UBC), and Eastern Mennonite University.

Last, but certainly not least I would like to thank Lois Gardner, who has encouraged me throughout this project. It was my good fortune to rent her suite and benefit from all that she has to offer.

My hope is that this book will help to clarify what genuine reconciliation entails, offer practical skills, and most importantly help strengthen and build networks to create conditions for a more peaceful and just world. To this end, I encourage any feedback about this book by e-mailing me at **jessie@worldviewstrategies.com**

TERMINOLOGY

Reconciliation

This book suggests the heart of reconciliation is a parallel process of personal and political transformation from systems of domination to relationships of mutuality. It also suggests four guiding touchstones needed to create conditions for reconciliation: drawing on the fundamental worldviews of the parties themselves, transcending the victim-offender cycle, engaging in large-scale social change, and assessing appropriate timing and tactics.

Worldviews

I use worldviews synonymously with other terms such as "worlds," "world frames," and "cosmology." I took my working definition from Thomas Berry who explains that worldviews are how a given culture sees its relationship to the rest of the universe, its creation at the beginning of time, and its beliefs about how human affairs should best fit into the bigger picture.[1]

Worldviewing Skills

Jayne Docherty argues metaphorically that a worldview is not a noun but rather a verb, as we are constantly in the process of "worldview formation, maintenance, and revision."[2] Similarly, Michelle LeBaron suggests that we should engage in a practice where we align and attune our worldview with our actions.[3] Given that reconciliation is about transitioning from systems of

---

[1] Thomas Berry in Baylands Production, "The Unfolding Story," (1993)

[2] Jayne Docherty, *Learning Lessons from Waco: When the Parties Bring Their Gods to the Negotiation Table* (Syracuse: Syracuse University Press, 2001), 50.

[3] Michelle LeBaron, *Bridging Cultural Conflicts: A New Approach for a Changing World* (San Francisco: Jossey Bass, 2003), 170.

domination to relationships of mutuality, I built on Docherty's concept of a verb to describe a set of "worldviewing skills" useful in creating conditions for reconciliation.

Worldview Pluralism

I draw on Raimon Panikkar's and Robert Vachon's understanding of pluralism. They write that "plurality" is a concept that reflects diverse and separate concepts that can be differentiated by logical thought. Pluralism, on the other hand, refers to a *radical diversity* that emphasizes the diversity in beliefs about our human relationship to the universe and how as humans we fit into the bigger picture.[4] Pluralism allows for coexistence between diverse relationships to truth and reality and the various ways human culture expresses these beliefs.

Worldview Rigidity and Worldview Flexibility

Mary Clark uses the term worldview rigidity and flexibility to describe a culture's capacity to adapt their worldview to changing circumstances over time. In this book, I also use worldview rigidity as a way to describe an automatic rejection of worldview difference. In this context, worldview flexibility is closely linked to worldview pluralism in that it is the capacity to be loyal to one's worldview and engage across worldview difference. I chose to use the terms worldview rigidity and flexibility in this book to be consistent with the other worldview terminology and overall concept of "worldviewing skills."

Western Culture

I draw on Kalpana Das' understanding of culture to include the fundamental worldview, the structural dimensions, and the more visible aspects such as customs, language, food,

---

[4] Robert Vachon, "Guswenta or the Intercultural Imperative (Continued) (Part I, Section Ii: A Common Horizon)," *Inter Culture* XXVIII, no. 3 (1995): 6-10.

habitation, and technology.[5] In this sense, and for the purposes of this book, "Western culture" does not refer to the diverse people living in the Western hemisphere, but rather the fundamental worldview expressed in the majority of Western institutions and ways of life. While Western culture has in the past been based on an Earth-centred and later a God-centred worldview, Thomas Berry describes its current foundations as human-centred, whereby the Earth is seen as primarily for human use.[6]

Re-civilizing Western Cultures

It is not my intention to suggest that "civilizations" are the ultimate way of organizing human affairs, but rather to highlight the distortion Western cultures have undergone in recent centuries and the need for a radical re-alignment between what we now know about the nature of the universe and how we organize human affairs accordingly. Moreover, in using the term "re-civilizing" I am situating our current state of affairs within the context of the disintegration and genesis of civilizations as described in Arnold Toynbee's work, *A Study of History*.[7] In this way, approaches to social change can be situated within the current context of the disintegration of the Enlightenment era. Consequently I am suggesting reconciliation as I describe it in this book as a theory of change to help nurture the genesis of a new era that is more in alignment with our current understanding of the universe and how best to organize human affairs accordingly.

---

[5] Das in Robert Vachon, "Guswenta or the Intercultural Imperative: Towards a Re-Enacted Peace Accord between the Mohawk Nation and the North American Nation-States (and Their People)," *Inter Culture* XXVIII, no. 127 (1995): 53.

[6] Tomas Berry, *The Great Work: Our Way into the Future* (New York: Bell Tower, 1999), 45 & 65.

[7] His work describes the genesis, growth, breakdown, and disintegration of civilizations throughout human history from around the world. See Arnold Toynbee, *A Study of History*, 10 vols. (London: Oxford University Press, 1955).

PART ONE

The Way In

CHAPTER 1

FOUR TOUCHSTONES
FOR RECONCILIATION

Times of transition are difficult to characterize and even more to name. Such times are half blind and half invisible, in as much as they represent a transition between what is old and familiar…and what is new and strange[8].

A global snapshot reveals that we live in truly remarkable times of transition and change. In 1989 Soviet rule in Eastern Europe ended, thus changing the bipolar climate that characterized the world order for the previous fifty years.[9] South America has gone through a dramatic shift in which

---

[8] Bonaventura De Sousa Santos, *Toward a New Legal Common Sense: Law, Globalization, and Emancipation* (London: Butterworths Lexis Nexis, 2002), xvi.

[9] Robert Schreiter, *Reconciliation: Mission & Ministry in a Changing Social Order* (New York: Orbis Books, 2002), 5.

democracies rather than dictatorships became the norm for the majority of its people.[10] In the wake of de-colonization in Africa, latent conflicts created by colonial regimes and suppressed by bi-polar tensions, have erupted throughout the continent.[11] Indigenous international relations has developed as a way to strengthen grassroots struggles for recognition, reparations for historical injustices, and just agreements on issues such as land and governance.[12] Most recently, political violence and the "war on terrorism" have created a new kind of bi-polar climate, fuelling in many cases victim-offender cycles.

Our current international system was designed for a world order based on Nation-State sovereignty. International conflict resolution mechanisms were created to help prevent and resolve wars between states, while generally disallowing international intervention in domestic issues. However, since the end of the Cold War and de-colonization, the majority of conflicts have shifted from those between states to conflicts that are predominantly intra-state. Consequently, international relations have become unresponsive to the majority of contemporary conflicts.[13]

Africa has seen some of the world's worst human tragedies; yet it has also seen unexpected miracles, such as the end of the apartheid era in South Africa in which Nelson

---

[10]Ibid.@8-9

[11] Ibid.@9: there have been over seventy coups during the first thirty years of independence, countless civil wars, and atrocities such as the Rwandan genocide.

[12] Elzar Barkan, *The Guilt of Nations: Restitution and Negotiating Historical Injustices* (Baltimore: The John Hopkins University Press, 2000), xxvi, Claude Denis, *We Are Not You: First Nations and Canadain Modernity* (Peterborough: Broadview press, 1997), 113.

[13]John Paul Lederach, *Building Peace: Sustainable Reconciliation in Divided Societies* (Washington D.C: United States Institute of Peace Press, 1997), 18, International Commission On Intervention and State Sovreignty, "The Responsibility to Protect: Report of the International Commission on Intervention on State Sovreignty," (Ottawa: International Development Research Centre, 2001), 3.

Mandela went from prisoner to president virtually overnight. Moreover, South Africa's Truth and Reconciliation Commission in 1994 has led the world away from retributive justice towards restorative justice that includes healing the past and social transformation. Since then, there has been a proliferation of transitional justice processes whose intent is to foster reconciliation throughout the world in such places as Peru, Bosnia-Herzogavina, Timor-Leste, Rwanda, Sierra Leone, Nigeria, and Cambodia.[14] Recently, Canada has begun to talk about reconciliation as a potential approach for First Nations – Canada conflict resolution. However, there has been no comprehensive study of what reconciliation means or entails.

Since there are hundreds of definitions of reconciliation, coming to a single definition is a complex and sometimes overwhelming task. A survey of the word "reconciliation," or similar corresponding concepts,[15] in a variety of languages illustrates the diversity found in its meaning. For example, the Inuit word *inuuqatigiikkannilirniq* means "people living together...in complete interdependence with each other and nature."[16] The Iroquois concept for peace and peaceful coexistence goes "beyond resolving conflicts to actively care for the other's welfare."[17] In Rwanda, reconciliation is "rooted in a metaphor that means to straighten crooked sticks so that there is a clear flow of energy between them."[18] Similarly, the

---

[14] International Centre for Transitional Justice, (2003 [cited December 10 2003]); available from http://www.ictj.org.

[15] R. Panikkar explains that it is not useful to merely translate words from one language to another. Rather it is important to find the corresponding concept or function. He calls this *homeomorphism*. See Robert Vachon, "Beyond the Religion of Human Rights, the Nation State, and the Rule of Law," *Inter Culture*, no. 143 (2002): 44.

[16] Vern Redekop, *From Violence to Blessing: How an Understanding of Deep-Rooted Conflict Can Open Paths to Reconciliation* (Ottawa: Novalis, 2002), 286.

[17] Ibid.; Alfred, Taiaiake, personal communication, January 14 2004.

[18] Ibid., 287.

ancient Greek word for reconciliation, *katallaso* refers to a "significant change within oneself to make appeasement or create a positive disposition toward the other."[19] The Greek root, *allaso*, suggests change or total transformation.[20] The composite Latin words *re* and *calare* literally means to "call together again or make friendly again."[21] In China, reconciliation is closely linked to the maintaining of social face (mien-tzu) through one's reputation and appearance; as well as honor (lien) reflecting one's conscience and integrity. A Chinese pastoral counsellor explains, "the wise person is like a vast ocean within, and nothing can stir or trouble the waters."[22] In Hebrew, *peshera* is synonymous to "making an agreement."[23] Finally, the word *Islam* literally "contains a theology of a reconciled humanity" by finding peace through surrender to God.[24]

Each culture provides a unique window into how it views reality and how best to maintain harmonious relations with others and the rest of creation. Various Indigenous teachings explain that there are four colours of people on Earth and that each group possesses unique gifts. In one Cree and Ojibway teaching, the people of the black colour hold the power of using sound for bringing new things into creation; the people of the red colour hold the knowledge of how human beings can live in harmony with the rest of creation; the people of the

---

[19] Ibid., 286.

[20] Sr Editor Mark Norris Eschatology Today, *Hunting for Key Words the Inductive Way* (2004 [cited January 22 2004]); available from www.eschatologytoday.net/keywordshtm.

[21] Redekop, *From Violence to Blessing: How an Understanding of Deep-Rooted Conflict Can Open Paths to Reconciliation*, 285.

[22] David Augsburger, *Conflict Mediation across Cultures: Pathways and Patterns* (Westminster: John Knox Press, 1992), 265.

[23] Redekop, *From Violence to Blessing: How an Understanding of Deep-Rooted Conflict Can Open Paths to Reconciliation*.

[24] Redmond Fitmaurice, "Other Religions and Reconciliation," in *Reconciliation in Religion and Society*, ed. Michael Hurley (Belfast: Queens University of Belfast, 1994), 166.

yellow colour possess knowledge about the inner workings of the human mind and body; and finally the people of the white colour's gift is that of communication enabling all of the four colour's gifts to be brought together.[25] Gifts attributed to each people differ depending on the Indigenous nation. What is important is not an essentialist notion of culture or race, but rather an understanding that each worldview contains unique gifts.

Similar teachings around the world echo the importance and richness of human diversity. Chiapas elder, Don Antonio explains, "there are many colors and ways of thinking in the world, and how happy the world will be when all the colors and ways of thinking have a place."[26] His words remind us that culture is more than diverse food, colourful dress, and complex languages. Knowledge systems about how the world is ordered and creation itself are embedded within every culture. When a language or culture is lost, we lose a piece of knowledge about life.[27] In this way, just as plant biodiversity is essential for the survival of the planet as a living entity, so is cultural diversity essential for the quality of human life and even its very survival.

While each culture has its own unique version of reconciliation, it is nonetheless possible to identify common themes in the various approaches. Genuine reconciliation involves a transition from systems of domination to relationships of mutuality. Consequently, genuine reconciliation also requires a parallel process of personal and political transformation.[28] Systems of domination come in a variety of forms, including

---

[25] Rupert Ross, *Returning to the Teachings: Exploring Aboriginal Justice* (Toronto: Penguin Books, 1996), 272-73.

[26] Subcommandante Marcos, *Our Word Is Our Weapon* (New York: Seven Stories Press, 2001), 375.

[27] Philip Coulter, "The End of the Wild," in *CBC Ideas* (Toronto: CBC Ideas, 2001).

[28] Redekop, *From Violence to Blessing: How an Understanding of Deep-Rooted Conflict Can Open Paths to Reconciliation*, 287, Walter Wink, *When the Powers Fall: Reconciliation in the Healing of Nations* (Minneapolis: Fortress Press: Minneapolis, 1998), 13.

totalitarian regimes, civil war, genocide, and internal colonialism in places like Canada, the United States, Australia, and New Zealand. While peace accords may mark an end to violence, experience demonstrates that unless personal and structural change follows, violence will quickly erupt again.[29]

In addition to fostering violence, systems of domination are also embedded in institutional structures and in the hearts and minds of the people. Because of the systemic nature of the problem, reconciliation is a whole-hearted process that involves both personal and societal engagement. This introductory chapter proposes four guiding touchstones for meaningful reconciliation: drawing on the worldviews of the parties themselves; transcending the victim-offender cycle; engaging in large-scale social change; and assessing timing and tactics. In this way, I lay the foundation for the remaining focus of this book: the importance of learning worldviewing skills to foster reconciliation.

Unfortunately, some who wish to hold on to power have misused the concept of reconciliation as a way to avoid accountability and prevent liberation. Others have internalised systems of domination to such an extent they end up falling short of the intended goals of reconciliation. In turn, these conditions have led to mistaken understandings of reconciliation and in some cases have increased oppression and violence. Similarly, reconciliation has been used falsely as a "quick fix" for historical and contemporary injustices. Part of the difficulties lies in the vague meanings given to the term. Consequently, many contemporary scholars begin any serious analysis of reconciliation with an exploration of false reconciliation, thus clearing the ground for a discussion of what contributes to genuine reconciliation.[30]

---

[29] John Paul Lederach, "Fundamentals of Peace-Building" (paper presented at the Eastern Mennonite University Conflict Transformation Program, Harrisonburg, January 6-10 2003).

[30] Stanley Cohen, *States of Denial: Knowing About Atrocities and Suffering* (Oxford: Blackwell Publishers, 2001), 238; Schreiter, *Reconciliation: Mission & Ministry in a Changing Social Order*, 18; Wink, *When the Powers Fall: Reconciliation in the Healing of Nations*, 24.

FALSE RECONCILIATION

Robert Schreiter identifies the following three understandings of reconciliation that distort and falsify its true meanings: reconciliation as a hasty process, reconciliation instead of liberation, and reconciliation as a managed process.[31]

Reconciliation as a Hasty Process

Reconciliation as a hasty process attempts to address historical injustices and suffering by suppressing its memory.[32] Generally those calling for this kind of reconciliation want victims to let "bygones be bygones" or to "turn the page and start afresh." Not surprisingly, it is usually the perpetrating group that espouses this approach. As they realize either the enormity of what they have done or become aware of the legal ramifications of their actions, they seek quick solutions by glossing over the past.[33]

This form of false reconciliation trivializes social suffering and avoids addressing the root causes of injustices. Glossing over the past ultimately gives a clear message that experiences of suffering are trivial, and therefore those that suffered themselves are unimportant to the process.[34] Memory, in fact, is closely linked to human identity[35] and dignity. In ignoring memory, human identity and dignity are likewise further eroded. As a result, far from reconciling relationships, this understanding of reconciliation entrenches injustice and solidifies a system of domination.[36]

---

[31] Schreiter, *Reconciliation: Mission & Ministry in a Changing Social Order*, 18.

[32] Ibid.

[33] Ibid., 19.

[34] Ibid.

[35] Human identity is considered a fundamental human need as it connects us to a larger community and fulfills the human psyche's need for meaning, belonging and connectedness. In *From Violence to Blessing: How An Understanding of Deep-rooted Conflict Can Open Paths to Reconciliation*, Vern Redekop summarizes the human identity needs debate and offers a new synthesis (see chapter 2, p.31-59.)

[36] Schreiter, *Reconciliation: Mission & Ministry in a Changing Social Order*, 18.

Quick apology/forgiveness tactics tend to dominate these attempts at reconciliation. For example, Canada, through the federal department – Indian and Northern Affairs (INAC), issued a statement of reconciliation. While many within INAC worked hard to produce this statement, this is a good example of how good intentions can still fall short of creating conditions for genuine reconciliation.[37] While this statement offers an apology[38] and is certainly an important step in the right direction, it frames the relationship with Indigenous peoples within the context of the Canadian state despite the fact that many Indigenous peoples continue to struggle for the status of autonomous nations. Moreover, the "apology" refers to the implementation of the residential schools system, but neglects to address the root causes of conflict, namely land, governance, justice, and cultural domination. Finally, the federal government sets the terms of the relationship instead of being open to a full and equal negotiation of it.

If Canada wanted to create conditions for genuine reconciliation it would be more appropriate to start with a statement of repentance[39] or recognition whereby it would acknowledge the damage it has done and commit to acting upon changing itself systemically.[40] There are no "easy shortcuts;" reconciliation is a complex process that requires time, personal commitment, political will, and resources.[41]

---

[37] See Appendix II

[38] See the following authors for more information regarding false versus authentic apologies: Janet Bavelas, "Aplogies, Responsibility, and Restorative Justice: The Role of Language" (paper presented at the Centre for Studies in Religion and Society, University of Victoria, November 21 2001); Aaron Lazare, "The Healing Power of Apology" (paper presented at the Agenda For Reconciliation, Caux, Switzerland, August 6 2002).

[39] Repentance is a general confession and involves three elements. First we are sorry for what we have done. Second we offer reparations for damage done by our sin. Third, we amend our life by making a commitment and intention to change. Bishop Hanen, October 31 2003.

[40]Schreiter, *Reconciliation: Mission & Ministry in a Changing Social Order*, 21.

[41] Mohammed Abu-Nimer, ed., *Reconciliation, Justice, and Coexistence* (Lanham: Lexington Books, 2001), 346.

Reconciliation Instead of Liberation

Strategies to prevent liberation can come under several pseudo-reconciliation guises. Their aim is almost always to avoid structural changes, deny accountability, and ultimately hold on to power. There are five predominant ways that reconciliation is used in this way: 1) calls for "peace", 2) compromise, 3) false "truth" processes, 4) neutrality, and 5) individualized approaches to reconciliation.

During revolutionary change, some leaders call for peace when in actual fact they mean, "the oppressed should not disturb the false tranquillity of a society built on violence."[42] For example, in the Philippines, small landowners of twelve acres would often find their land encroached on by large landowners. The typical cycle of injustice, revolt, and repression would ensue. Eventually, the small landowners would receive letters to attend a meeting with the barrio captain (who is linked to the government) and his/her antagonist. The barrio captain's job was to help the two parties "reconcile." The problem; however, was always presented as a communication breakdown or a relationship in need of healing rather than addressing the injustice. Small landowners were cajoled into shaking hands with their oppressors without any change to the injustice of land encroachment.[43]

Similarly, genuine reconciliation "can be subverted by a government propaganda apparatus that equates reconciliation with compromise, the toleration of injustice, and obedience to the higher powers."[44] For example, treaty negotiations in British Columbia use interest-based negotiation modelled on Fisher and Ury's *Getting to Yes* model. Rather than addressing land encroachment and Indigenous nationhood, the discussions are focused on how to best use the land so that everyone's needs are accommodated. Furthermore, as a pre-requisite, Indigenous people must agree to claim no more than five to

---

[2] Wink, *When the Powers Fall: Reconciliation in the Healing of Nations*, 26.

[43] Ibid., 24-25.

[44] Ibid., 26.

eight percent of their traditional territory. In many cases, the processes themselves are designed in a way that ultimately avoids accountability for key issues and prevents veritable justice.[45] It is no surprise that under these circumstances treaty talks are often riddled with difficulty.[46]

Some "truth" processes give the illusion of attempting to address the root causes of injustice; however in reality it is merely another tactic to hold on to power and avoid accountability. For example, immediately following El Salvador's truth commission report that identified over forty high level officials responsible for serious human rights abuses, the president of El Salvador presented a bill, that was quickly accepted by parliament, granting a blanket amnesty for all perpetrators named in the report. This was seen by many human rights activists as a tactic intentionally used to weaken the judiciary and avoid holding perpetrators accountable for their crimes.[47] Since then, structural violence in El Salvador has deepened resulting in a crime rate that sees as many deaths as during the civil war.[48] In other words, truth was sought and then promptly shelved. Archbishop Desmond Tutu insists, "that unless there is real material transformation in the lives of those who have been...victims, we might as well kiss reconciliation goodbye."[49]

---

[45] Chrisjohn, et al. *The Circle Game: Shadows and Substance in Indian Residential School Experience in Canada* (Penticton: Theylus Books ltd., 1997), 105.

[46] See the following texts for a more comprehensive analysis: Taiaiake Alfred, *Deconstructing the British Columbia Treaty Process* (2000 [cited November 15 2003]); available from http://taiaiake.com/words/; James Tully, "Reconsidering the B.C. Treaty Process" (paper presented at the Speaking Truth To Power: A Treaty Forum, Ottawa, December 1 2003).

[47] Priscilla Hayner, *Unspeakable Truths: Confronting State Terror and Atrocity* (New York: Routledge, 2001), 91-93.

[48] Hizkias Assefa, "Philosophy and Praxis of Reconciliation" (paper presented at the Eastern Mennonite University Summer Peace-building Institute, Harrisonburg, May 16-24 2002).

[49] Desmond Tutu, *No Future without Forgiveness* (New York: Doubleday, 1997), 229.

Neutrality in the context of injustice merely perpetuates oppression and certainly does not lead to genuine reconciliation.[50] For example, a South African church officer insisted throughout the apartheid era "the duty of the churches is to be agents of reconciliation. That means we must avoid taking sides and be neutral."[51] In reality many deep-rooted conflicts require an acceleration of conflict "as a necessary stage in forcing those in power to bring about genuine change and ultimately reconciliation."[52]

A final reconciliation approach that avoids liberation and falls short of its intended goals is focusing on individual reconciliation without equal attention being given to structural changes. For example, the new Alternative Dispute Resolution framework to address residential school grievances in Canada focuses on individual settlements for survivors who experienced physical and sexual abuse but does not, as yet, address deeper structural issues, namely systemic cultural domination, intergenerational trauma, and collective denial. While settlements often partially fulfill the human need for justice and certainly can contribute to reconciliation, they cannot replace liberation from systems of domination, a crucial precondition for meaningful and lasting reconciliation. Otherwise, reconciliation would simply mean, "that one side gets the power and the other side gets reconciled to it".[53]

Reconciliation as a Managed Process
Sometimes reconciliation is confused with mediation and other conflict resolution techniques. In this view, a skilled mediator helps conflicting parties address underlying interests and values in their conflict. Subsequently, an agreement

---

[50] Wink, *When the Powers Fall: Reconciliation in the Healing of Nations*, 26.

[51] Kraybill in Ibid.

[52] Lederach, *Building Peace: Sustainable Reconciliation in Divided Societies*, 65; Wink, *When the Powers Fall: Reconciliation in the Healing of Nations*, 26.

[53] Alinsky, *Rules for Radicals: A Pragmatic Primer for Realistic Radicals*, 13.

is reached.[54] Such a process is certainly not hasty and has similarities with reconciliation such as the acknowledgement of legitimate interests and human dignity. Nonetheless, it reduces reconciliation to a mere technical skill. Robert Schreiter argues that reconciliation is more of an attitude, way of life, or spiritual stance than a mechanistic tool to develop.[55] In this view, reconciliation cannot be managed, forced or predicted. Conditions can be created to foster reconciliation, but a given process cannot guarantee it.

Hizkias Assefa suggests conflict-handling approaches that foster mutual participation are the most likely to create conditions for reconciliation. He, therefore, places conflict-handling approaches on a spectrum reflecting the degree of mutual participation parties have in their search for mutually agreeable solutions. In this way, Assefa explains reconciliation as a paradigm shift from coercive force to voluntarism and from staunch individualism to interdependence and mutuality. He has developed the following diagram to illustrate this continuum and underlying values of participation.[56]

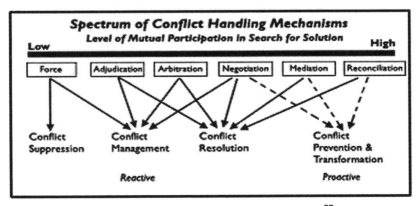

Figure 1: Reconciliation as a continuum[57]

[54] Schreiter, *Reconciliation: Mission & Ministry in a Changing Social Order*, 25.

[55] Ibid., 25-26.

[56] Hizkias Assefa, "The Meaning of Reconciliation," in *People Building Peace: 35 Inspiring Stories from around the World*, ed. European Centre for Conflict Prevention (Utrecht: European Centre for Conflict Prevention, 1999), 37.

[57] Ibid., 35. Reprinted with permission of the author; see Appendix IV.

At the left hand of the spectrum, force reflects an approach where one party imposes its solution on another and consequently mutual participation is minimal or non-existent. Solutions imposed by force generally last until "the vanquished is able to muster sufficient force to reverse the situation."[58] Next along the continuum is adjudication. Rather than an adversary imposing a solution, a third party does. The level of party participation increases in that parties can present their position and reasoning as they advocate their ideal solution. Ultimately, however, a third party makes a final decision that is enforced by law.[59] A little further to the right is arbitration, where the parties themselves rather than the state select the third party. Additionally, the parties can decide on what basis the decision will be made and can also agree to whether or not the outcome will be binding. Nonetheless, a third party decides the final outcome and, depending on what kind of arbitration is used, it can be binding by law.[60] Adjudication and arbitration are rarely effective conflict-handling approaches because the losing party tends to either engage in endless appeals or refuses to cooperate in the implementation process.[61] Thus, conflict management approaches such as force, adjudication, and arbitration attempt to control or mitigate the destructive elements of conflict but do not address the root causes.[62]

Continuing to the right, negotiation is a conflict handling approach where all parties are actively engaged in the search for a solution. While the parties themselves formulate and work towards solutions that are mutually agreeable, in practice the party with the most power tends to have more leverage and hence tends to benefit the most.[63] Mediation is

---

[58] Ibid., 39.

[59] Ibid., 37.

[60] Ibid., 38.

[61] Ibid., 39.

[62] Ibid.

[63] Ibid., 37.

similar to negotiation; however a third party facilitates the process to help decrease the impact of obstacles such as power imbalances and destructive communication patterns. The mediator, unlike the adjudicator, facilitates the process while the parties themselves remain in charge of formulating the issues, coming up with solutions, and committing to implementation for conflict prevention.[64] However, the problem with conflict resolution approaches such as mediation and negotiation is that they are frequently embedded within a dominant Western worldview and can lead to culturally inappropriate solutions in many contexts. Moreover, these approaches are primarily re-active rather than preventative or transformative.[65]

To the far right, Assefa places reconciliation within a conflict transformation approach. For Assefa, reconciliation reflects a conflict handling approach that has the highest degree of mutual participation as it works to address the root causes of conflict and endeavours to transform relationships from that of resentment and hostility to co-existence, mutuality, and eventually even friendship. Consequently, "parties must be equally invested and participate intensively in the reconciliation process."[66] The reconciliation of a social order requires a commitment to personal and societal transformation by all concerned.[67] In this way, reconciliation is more voluntary and internal than externally forced, managed, or predicted.

Rather than seeing reconciliation as a managed process, it is more useful to consider how conditions can be created to foster increased participation, encourage mutuality, and inspire personal and societal transformation. In this way, various conflict handling approaches can be useful at various stages of a conflict only if they are understood as tools to foster mutuality and ultimately create conditions for reconcilia-

---

[64] Ibid., 38.

[65] Ibid., 39.

[66] Ibid.

[67] Ibid.

tion. For example, Maggie Hodgson explains the Baxter class action case is being used by residential school survivors as a way to force the federal government to accept responsibility for cultural domination not as an end in and of itself, but rather as a stepping stone for creating conditions for fair dialogue, just settlement, and transforming our social order from that of cultural domination to mutuality.[68]

Lederach uses the metaphor of a process-structure to shed light on all the various peace-building activities, how they fit together, and hopefully create conditions for lasting reconciliation. A process structure is a term frequently used in quantum physics, chaos theory, and complexity science to explain a phenomenon that is simultaneously a process and a structure. For example, if you stand in a river, you see water constantly moving but don't necessarily see the river as a whole. From an airplane you can see the structure of the river, but you can't see the movement of the water. Similarly peace-building is simultaneously a process and a structure. Lederach explains you need a vision or loose structure but you also need peace-building activities and processes as a way to hold both together.[69] In consequence, I propose the four guiding touchstones described below when considering strategies and peace building activities to foster genuine reconciliation.

GENUINE RECONCILIATION

Genuine reconciliation is a paradigmatic shift that involves transitioning from systems of domination to relationships of mutuality.[70] Engaging in a parallel process of personal and societal change, reconciliation has the potential to lead us

---

[68]For greater details see Maggie Hodgson, "Residential School: 'A Shared Journey' in Redefining Relationships," (Edmonton: 2003).

[69] Lederach, "Fundamentals of Peace-Building".

[70]Redekop, *From Violence to Blessing: How an Understanding of Deep-Rooted Conflict Can Open Paths to Reconciliation*, 287; Wink, *When the Powers Fall: Reconciliation in the Healing of Nations*, 13.

through our current global crisis into not merely a new world order but more importantly into a very different world and relationships. I suggest the following four guiding touchstones for creating conditions for lasting reconciliation: drawing on the fundamental worldviews of the parties' themselves; transcending the victim-offender cycle; engaging all sectors of society in large-scale social change; and finally assessing timing and tactics.

1. Drawing on the fundamental worldviews of the parties themselves

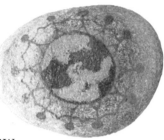

Most peace-building and reconciliation literature addresses culture or the underlying worldviews of the parties as an additional element to consider. In this book, I argue that drawing on the culture and worldviews of the parties themselves lays both the relational foundation for reconciliation, as well as offers a wellspring for personal and cultural regeneration. While the current need for reconciliation is global, an international template is doomed to fail. It would be irrelevant to many people and cultures; more importantly it would risk reinforcing cultural domination worldwide. One of the most pernicious aspects of systems of domination, and hence deep-rooted conflict, is the imposition of one worldview on another.[71]

Being aware of one's culture is a little like being a fish in water. Although culture is "all pervasive," we are seldom aware of its presence or importance. Various metaphors, such as this one, help describe different aspects of culture.[72] The

---

[71] Taiaiake Alfred, *Peace, Power, and Righteousness: an Indigenous manifesto* (Don Mills: Oxford University Press, 1999), 2; Mary Clark, *In Search of Human Nature* (New York: Routledge, 2002), 237; Marcos, *Our Word Is Our Weapon*, 116, Nudler, "On Conflicts and Metaphors," 118.

[72] LeBaron, *Bridging Cultural Conflicts: A New Approach for a Changing World*, 23.

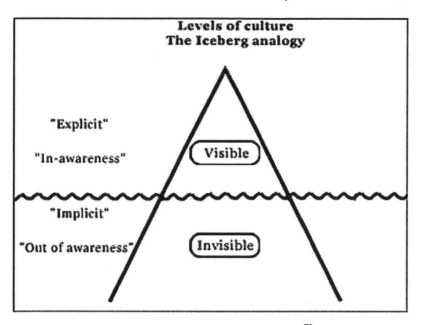

Figure 2: The Iceberg Analogy[73]

iceberg analogy, for example, illustrates the visible and invisible aspects of culture.[74] The most visible parts of culture – such as language, dress, food, literature, and art – merely represent the tip of the iceberg, constituting only ten percent of the totality of a culture (See Figure 2).[75] Below the surface, and therefore less visible, are the most significant aspects of culture such as concepts of justice, gender roles, ideals of childrearing, notions about logic validity, power, leadership, and morality reside. These elements represent the remaining ninety percent of what culture entails.

Kalpana Das extends our understanding of the iceberg

---

[73] Das in Ibid. Adapted with permission of the author; see Appendix IV.

[74] Vachon, "Guswenta or the Intercultural Imperative: Towards a Re-Enacted Peace Accord between the Mohawk Nation and the North American Nation-States (and Their People)," 52.

[75] Ibid.

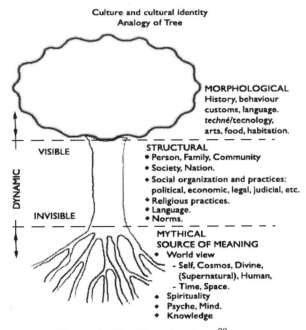

Figure 3: The Tree Analogy[80]

image by employing the tree analogy to emphasize levels of stability and consistency within cultures (see Figure 3).[76] For Das, the roots of the tree symbolize the matrix or underlying worldview of a culture and does not change as easily as the structural dimensions (the trunk) or the morphological dimensions (the foliage). The matrix or fundamental worldview is essentially how a given culture sees its relationship to the rest of the universe, its creation at the beginning of time, and its beliefs about how best to organize human affairs accordingly.[77] The trunk of the tree is analogous to a culture's institutions or structural arrangements such as systems of

---

[76] Ibid., 52.

[77] Thomas Berry in Baylands Production, "The Unfolding Story, " (1993); Vachon, "Guswenta or the Intercultural Imperative: Towards a Re-Enacted Peace Accord between the Mohawk Nation and the North American Nation-States (and Their People)," 53.

governance, economics, justice, health, education, and religious practices.[78] These structures simultaneously reflect, reinforce, teach and legitimise a culture's worldview. [79]

Finally, the foliage of the tree is similar to the tip of the iceberg, representing things like the arts, language, and dress. The tree analogy shows that the most important part of culture is its worldview as it is the foundation and nourishment that feeds a society's institutions and gives meaning to the more visible parts of culture such as food, language, and the arts.

Oscar Nudler, an Argentinian worldview conflict theorist, explains the importance of worldviews for human survival. He cites, "worldviews fulfil the most general set of pre-understanding one has about reality."[81] Worldviews, he continues, are rooted in our most fundamental human need for meaning and are actually critical for survival. Mary Clark, biologist and conflict theorist, echoes his words, explaining that the human psyche needs a set of beliefs to make meaning out of its existence.[82] Nudler argues, "depriving people of their worlds and colonizing their minds for the sake of the

---

[78] Vachon, "Guswenta or the Intercultural Imperative: Towards a Re-Enacted Peace Accord between the Mohawk Nation and the North American Nation-States (and Their People)."

[79] For example, a culture that holds a polarized worldview of good and evil may develop a justice system that punishes wrongdoers. On the other hand a worldview that sees the humanity in all may regard wrongdoing as a reflection of social ills, and as a result design justice processes that focus on healing, accountability, and social change. See Ross, *Returning to the Teachings: Exploring Aboriginal Justice*, 5; Sutherland, *Colonialism, Crime, and Dispute Resolution: A Critical Analysis of Canada's Aboriginal Justice Strategy*.

[80] Das in Vachon, "Guswenta or the Intercultural Imperative: Towards a Re-Enacted Peace Accord between the Mohawk Nation and the North American Nation-States (and Their People)," 53. Reprinted by permission of the author; see Appendix IV.

[81] P.A Heelan, *Space, Perception and the Philosophy of Sciences* (Berkely: University of California Press, 1983), 10, in Nudler, "On Conflicts and Metaphors."

[82] Clark, *In Search of Human Nature*, 235.

expansion of one particular world...represents an extreme form of oppression, probably harder to face than pure economic exploitation." [83]

Guatemalan Indigenous activist Rigoberta Menchu uses a tree metaphor to explain the resiliency of worldviews despite cultural oppression. On receiving the Alternative Peace prize, she addressed the audience and spoke of the impact of imperialism and colonization on her people. She said, "you have taken away the foliage and branches and even the trunk of our (cultural) tradition, but we still have our roots."[84] Her assertion that the roots remain despite the absence of the trunk and the foliage points to the tremendous adaptability of culture and its capacity to remain in the hearts and minds of the people regardless of the changing circumstances.[85]

Deep-rooted conflicts stemming from fundamental worldview differences between conflicting parties or groups are the most difficult and challenging to solve.[86] Nudler demonstrates how factual evidence cannot solve these disputes. For

Figure 4: The antelope/pelican ambiguous figure[87]

---

[83] Nudler, "On Conflicts and Metaphors," 188.

[84] Esteva, "Enough, Basta," 84 in Vachon, "Guswenta or the Intercultural Imperative: Towards a Re-Enacted Peace Accord between the Mohawk Nation and the North American Nation-States (and Their People)," 54.

[85] Docherty 2001, 2.

[86] Redekop, *From Violence to Blessing: How an Understanding of Deep-Rooted Conflict Can Open Paths to Reconciliation*, 33.

[87] Nudler, "On Conflicts and Metaphors," 198. Reprinted by permission of the publisher; see Appendix V.

example, one party looking at the gestalt ambiguous figure on the previous page may see an antelope, the other a pelican.

Neither are wrong; however in many worldview conflicts "people may refuse to accept that their (perspective) is just one... and that there may be other equally respectable alternatives."[88] This collision of worldviews can create an existential and identity crisis as it offers parties an alternative way to make meaning and perceive reality.[89] Rather than facing the internal dissonance this produces, many groups dismiss the other group as inferior or less than human, quickly entrenching stranger or even enemy images of one another.[90]

Worldview recognition is a fundamental human identity need.[91] In fact, a lack of recognition for worldview difference is so significant that many people will fight with their lives and the lives of others in its defence. For example, Subcommandante Marcos explains why the Chiapas have retreated to the mountains, risking their lives to defend their worldview and dignity:

> *We went to the mountains to find ourselves and see*
> *if we could ease the pain of being forgotten like*
> *stones and weeds.*[92]

In a letter to Leonard Peltier, Marcos wrote about their common "struggle for recognition and respect for the first inhabitants of the land."[93] For Marcos their struggle is about the "right to live or die according to our ideals."[94] Clark argues that most violent conflicts throughout history have

---

[88] Ibid., 181.

[89] Redekop, *From Violence to Blessing: How an Understanding of Deep-Rooted Conflict Can Open Paths to Reconciliation*, 34.

[90] Nudler, "On Conflicts and Metaphors," 198.

[91] Redekop, *From Violence to Blessing: How an Understanding of Deep-Rooted Conflict Can Open Paths to Reconciliation*, 35.

[92] Marcos, *Our Word Is Our Weapon*, 109.

[93] Ibid., 204.

[94] Ibid., 265.

been over meaning rather than scarce resources.[95] Moreover, many contemporary violent conflicts are within states between groups that hold different worldviews.[96] Consequently, learning how to dynamically engage across worldview difference and create shared pictures is a critical skill in today's world.[97]

Worldview conflict theorist, Jayne Docherty challenges us to think of worldviews not as a noun but rather as a verb. Worldviewing, Docherty argues, describes more accurately the process of "worldview formation, maintenance, and revision" that all human beings engage in throughout life.[98] Given that cultures, and hence worldviews, are constantly adapting to our environment Michelle LeBaron suggests engaging in a praxis where we continually align and attune our actions with our worldview.[99]

LeBaron sheds light on the dynamics of culture and conflict. She explains, "culture is like an underground river; it is full of life, dynamic, and powerful in shaping the course of conflicts, yet often outside our awareness."[100] Since we are all like fish swimming in our respective cultural waters, we seldom notice our own cultural lens until we bump into someone else's. By this time, we are often already in the full throes of conflict.[101]

Wade Davies argues that the twentieth century will be remembered, not for technological advancement, but rather

---

[95] Clark, *In Search of Human Nature*, 60.

[96] Lederach, *Building Peace: Sustainable Reconciliation in Divided Societies*, 18, Vamik Volkan, *Blood Lines: From Ethnic Pride to Ethnic Terrorism* (Boulder: Westview Press, 1997), 3-18.

[97] LeBaron, *Bridging Cultural Conflicts: A New Approach for a Changing World*, 291.

[98] Docherty, *Learning Lessons from Waco: When the Parties Bring Their Gods to the Negotiation Table*, 50.

[99] LeBaron, *Bridging Cultural Conflicts: A New Approach for a Changing World*, 170.

[100] Ibid., 3.

[101] Ibid., 275.

for the destruction of cultural diversity around the world. He explains, "we are living through a period of time where literally half of humanity's knowledge has been lost."[102] For example, at the beginning of the twentieth century over 6,000 languages were spoken, now over half of those languages are no longer taught to school children and therefore are effectively dead.[103] Consequently, we have already "lost half of the total knowledge of our species."[104]

For example, a turning point for Ardyth Cooper, of the T'Sou-ke nation,[105] occurred when she discovered that in her Indigenous language there is a specific name for the rain that comes during the late summer or early fall. "This rain is the rain that comes to help the elk wash the velvet off their antlers."[106] For Cooper, understanding this word provided an insight into the "deep connection between language, the land, the animals, her community and the interdependence between them all."[107] And most profoundly the way in which language recognizes the interconnectedness of all of these elements. As a consequence, she feels that in losing a language, many Indigenous people may lose knowledge about the interconnectedness of all these elements and consequently lose important local knowledge as well as the bedrock for Indigenous governance and justice institutions, which are based on the human responsibility to live in interdependence with all of creation.[108]

Loss of language has been but one aspect of our current global cultural crisis. Davies explains that cultures are always in the process of change and are able to adapt when the change has been on their own terms. "Cultures only

---

[102] Coulter, "The End of the Wild," 81.

[103] Ibid.

[104] Ibid.

[105] an Indigenous community in British Columbia

[106] Ardyth Cooper, personal communication, September 2003.

[107] Ibid.

[108] Cooper.

disappear when they're confronted by forces beyond their imaginings that lead to cataclysmic consequences." [109] Five hundred years of colonialism throughout various regions of the world; current multinational economic interests that devastate entire communities such as the Penan in southeast Asia where timber interests have changed the landscape and people forever; and cocaine cartels in places like Columbia exemplify forces that cultures cannot embrace and are likely to result in either assimilation or total annihilation.[110]

Taiaiake Alfred explains that seeking independence from colonial rule has been such a long and arduous struggle that many Indigenous people have felt that ridding themselves of foreign rule was an end in and of itself.[111] However, this is only the first step. According to Alfred, after independence has been gained, there remains the hard work of shifting from foreign institutions, based on Western models of governance, justice, and education, to creating institutions and structures that reflect the worldviews/cultures of Indigenous people.[112]

Western institutions are used in virtually every country, despite the dissonance with the worldviews of the people themselves. Indigenous scholar, Leroy Little Bear, explains that this dissonance leads to "jagged worldviews" – a kind of internal fragmentation where random pieces of puzzles from different world frames collide.[113] For example, the 1993 Report of Grand Council Treaty Number 3, explains how Indigenous and Euro-Canadian notions of justice collide. It states, "justice in the English lexicon ... means the system of law, courts, penal and appeal procedures of the Euro-Canadian system. There is no direct relationship with our systems. Justice to our people means allegiance to the integrity of our

---

[109] Coulter, "The End of the Wild," 18.

[110] Ibid.

[111] Taiaiake Alfred, (Camosun College, March 18th 2002).

[112] Alfred, *Peace, Power, and Righteousness: an indigenous manifesto,* xiv, 2.

[113] Leroy Little Bear, "Jagged Worldviews Colliding," in *Reclaiming Indigenous Voice and Vision,* ed. Marie Battiste (Vancouver: UBC Press, 2000), 84.

spiritual principles and values. Simple in meaning, but difficult to practice; to be pursued rather than attained…"[114] Maintaining a just social order for many Indigenous people involves having peaceful relationships with oneself, with other human beings, with the Creator, and with all of creation.[115] It follows that the imposition of Western institutions has led to worldview confusion, dissonance, and alienation, which in turn has fostered violence and other social dysfunctions such as addictions, high crime and suicide rates.[116] In fact, Alfred explains, "material poverty and social dysfunction are merely the visible surface of a deep pool of internal suffering. The underlying cause of that suffering is alienation – separation from our heritage and from ourselves."[117] Describing the effect that this has on many Indigenous people in Canada, Alfred writes, "there is more than one Indian in this world who dreams in the language of his ancestors and wakes mute to them, who dreams of peace and wakes to a deep and heavy anger."[118]

Hizkias Assefa, Ethiopian scholar and practitioner of national reconciliation processes, echoes Alfred's words as he shows how the dissonance between Western institutions and African culture can fuel ethnic conflict. He points out that while Western multi party electoral politics may work well in the resource-rich West and where the culture of individualism is valued, in Africa it actually worsens ethnic divisions and further erodes local culture. For example, in the wake of colonialism many African nations are deeply divided by ethnic strife and struggle for basic survival needs.

---

[114] Ross, *Returning to the Teachings: Exploring Aboriginal Justice*, 257.

[115] Alfred, *Peace, Power, and Righteousness: an indigenous manifesto*, 42; George Erasmus, *Third Annual Lafontaine-Baldwin Lecture* (2002 [cited March 16 2002]); available from http://cbc.ca/news/indepth/lafontaine_lectures/.

[116] Alfred, *Peace, Power, and Righteousness: an indigenous manifesto*, xv.

[117] Ibid.

[118] Ibid., 30.

Under these circumstances, some ethnic groups use their identity as political platforms against their enemy ethnic group and fight for resources along ethnic lines. Both Assefa and Taiaiake advocate for revitalizing local governance and dispute resolution processes that reflect the cultural norms of the people themselves.[119] Otherwise, Alfred argues, "the whole of the decolonisation process will have been for nothing if Indigenous government has no meaningful Indigenous character."[120]

Western culture, in its quest to expand its worldview and increase its economic resources, has become distorted and in equal need of regeneration. For example, Western notions of the individual which originally celebrated every human being's innate creativity and right to freedom has been overdeveloped at the expense of other equally important human needs such as for meaning and connectedness.[121] Moreover, unbridled individualism and technological "advancement" has resulted into an insatiable greed and self-absorption even at the expense of harming others and the Earth.[122]

Mary Clark explains, "in place of a transcendent myth, any emotionally satisfying narrative that speaks to our humanity, we have created a materialistic religion that leaves us, as people, empty of an emotionally satisfying, shared purpose."[123] Clark argues that this lack of meaningful purpose poses high stress on human beings and "may well be responsible for most fatal attack on others (murder) and on self (suicides), as well as for the much more frequent instances of lesser violence."[124]

---

[119] Ibid., xiv, Assefa, "Peace and Reconciliation as a Paradigm: A Philosophy of Peace and Its Implications on Conflict, Governance and Economic Growth," 30.

[120] Alfred, *Peace, Power, and Righteousness: an indigenous manifesto*, xiv.

[121] Clark, *In Search of Human Nature*, 233.

[122] Ibid., 306.

[123] Clark, *In Search of Human Nature*, 236.

[124] Clark, *In Search of Human Nature*, 246.

Recently, the *American Commission On Children At Risk*[125] completed a study linking youth suicide, crime, emotional problems, and violence to the lack of spiritual meaning in the lives of American youth. The report found that as humans we are "hardwired" for moral and spiritual meaning. Our brain is in fact "organized to ask ultimate questions and seek ultimate answers." Questions such as: "Why am I here" "What is my life's purpose?" "How should I live?" "What happens when I die?" The study argued that neglecting such spiritual needs creates a void, leading to social pathologies such as violence, crime, addictions, and excessive consumerism. The report's recommendations include encouraging spiritual values, pluralism, and community in American families, schools, and youth organizations.[126] Like Indigenous people, Westerners are experiencing profound dissonance between their worldview and their institutions. Mary Clark explains that a "culture that fails to change its perception on how to live" eventually self-destructs.[127] Therefore change must first start with the consciousness of individuals for a cohesive Western culture to regenerate and re-civilize itself.

Given the global loss of meaning in people's lives, it should be of no surprise that we have consequently lost a reverence for life. Global Action to Prevent War "claims that the last century was the most lethal in human history: over 200 million people were killed in 250 wars and genocidal onslaughts, more people than were killed in warfare in the past two thousand years."[128] In examining current wars

---

[125] The Commission was comprised of leading U.S children's doctors – The Commission On Children At Risk, *Hardwired to Connect: The New Scientific Case for Authoritative Communities* (2003 [cited November 15 2003]); available from http://americanvalues.org/html/hardwired.html.

[126] Ibid..

[127] Clark, *In Search of Human Nature*, 283.

[128] Global Action to Prevent War, ([cited November 15 2003]); available from www.globalactionpw.org. cited in Ben Hoffman, "Eliminating Organized Violence," (Metford: 2003), 7.

Lederach notes that over one third involve member-states of the United Nations, two thirds involve child soldiers, and "half of the current wars have been under way for more than a decade, and one-quarter of them for more than two decades."[129]

Unfortunately, in our haste to create order out of chaos, the international community implements solutions that may inadvertently create further cultural dissonance and erode the very capacities for peace already existing within cultures.[130] For example, in Sierra Leone the international community has imposed a Special Court and a Truth and Reconciliation Commission (TRC) as a way to assist in making the transition from civil war to peace and democracy. Sam Doe, director of the West African Network for Education and Peace (WANEP) explains that these foreign institutions may have laudable goals, however their mechanisms are not connected to Sierra Leonean culture, in which elders and chieftains typically play a central role in reconciliation and dispute resolution. Not only are these international institutions disconnected from the fundamental worldview of the people involved, many victims themselves do not understand the structures. As such, they are made to feel more like spectators to a peace process, and the vengeance that is lodged in their hearts and minds remains, ready to re-ignite at any time.[131]

Moreover, the international community tends to be crisis-driven and lacks a commitment to sustain support for such initiatives in the long term. Parachuting in with claims to bring peace and justice often raises the expectations of victims. When international interveners leave and there has been no real change, the psychological impact on victims can

---

[129] Lederach, *Building Peace: Sustainable Reconciliation in Divided Societies*, 4.

[130] Sam Gbaydee and Bombande Doe, Emmanuel Habuka, "A View from West Africa," in *A Handbook of International Peace-building*, ed. John Paul and Jenner Lederach, Janice (San Francisco: Jossey-Bass, 2002), 168.

[131] Ibid.

be devastating.[132] In fact, for some Sierra Leoneans, the imposition of a Special Court and Truth and Reconciliation Commission is seen as a way to give high paying jobs to people in the international community, rather than doing any good for Sierra Leone.

Mozambique, on the other hand, decided against using a truth commission in the aftermath of its war. Instead, it drew on its peoples' own healers and sets of beliefs to deal with the trauma and destruction of social cohesion. Community healers provide special ceremonies for those coming back home from war. It is believed that if you have murdered someone, their spirit remains attached to your shoulders. The ceremony removes the attached spirit and cleanses the person so that they are able to become human again. In addition, child soldiers must first live with elders before they are allowed to reintegrate into their home community. These ceremonies help combatants regain their humanity as well as offer spiritual reconciliation between the living and the dead.[133]

The question becomes how can we respond to the current global crisis in a way "that is neither derived from the Western model nor a simple reaction against it?" [134] Understanding the link between the global loss of meaning and current levels of violence is key when considering social change, conflict resolution, and ultimately reconciliation. Fuad Nahdi suggests that we are not experiencing a clash of civilizations but rather a mutual collapse of civilizations.[135] He argues we are "witness to the decay and failure of ingredients which made us 'civilized' in the first place."[136] Being civilized, Nahdi claims, is not "the rampant gluttony and crass materialism that dominates our high streets or the civil disorder and chaos in our cities;" nor is it defending against these vices

---

[132] Ibid., 169.

[133] Hayner, *Unspeakable Truths*, 116.

[134] Alfred, *Peace, Power, and Righteousness: an indigenous manifesto*, xviii.

[135] Fuad Nahdi, "Collapse of Civilizations," *For A Change* 16, no. 5 (2003).

[136] Ibid.

with "the perpetuation of distortions and half-truths... things like violence, dishonesty, lack of accountability and extremism."[137] For Nahdi, being civilised is based on five values – generosity, integrity, loyalty, honesty, and (inter) dependency.[138] Seen in this light, the most effective way to address our current global crisis is to surrender to the ending of our civilizations and to prepare for the rebirth of stronger and of more resilient civilizations. To accomplish this Nahdi suggests we need to "re-discover our essential humanity" and our relationship to the rest of creation.[139] Similarly, Lakota storyteller Joseph Marshall explains that the most effective way to regenerate culture, and hence prepare for our emerging civilizations, is to live our values and share our stories of virtues and those of our ancestors, as they contain the "core of cultural renewal for each new generation."[140]

Consequently, worldviewing skills that can foster reconciliation include understanding that all interventions are embedded in culture. Therefore we must develop strategies that strengthen personal integrity, cultural consistency, and local capacity. As we learn the power of personal integrity rather than coercive force, we not only re-create our cultures but also begin to regain our humanity. Moreover, developing intercultural skills, assessing and analysing conflict from a worldview lens, and deepening our understanding of the fundamental human need for meaning,[141] we not only learn how to engage across worldview difference but also deepen our own cultural roots and understanding about life itself.

---

[137] Ibid.

[138] Ibid.

[139] Ibid.

[140] Joseph Marshall, *The Lakota Way: Stories and Wisdom for Living* (New York: Penguin Books, 2001), xiv.

[141] Clark, *In Search of Human Nature*, 236; LeBaron, *Bridging Cultural Conflicts: A New Approach for a Changing World*, 32; Nudler, "On Conflicts and Metaphors," 191; Redekop, *From Violence to Blessing: How an Understanding of Deep-Rooted Conflict Can Open Paths to Reconciliation*, 34.

Finally, given that a fundamental characteristic of the ending of civilizations[142] and deep-rooted conflict is the erosion of people's meaning-making systems, worldview regeneration, revision, and alignment are necessary in any meaningful reconciliation initiatives. In fact, drawing on the fundamental worldviews of the parties involved provides the nourishment for the remaining three touchstones to create conditions for reconciliation: transcending the victim-offender cycle, engaging in large-scale social change, and finally assessing timing and tactics.

2. Transcending the Victim-Offender Cycle

Systems of domination inherently foster perpetual victim-offender cycles between groups and within groups themselves (see Appendix III). In fact the victim-offender paradigm becomes so internalized that strategies to end oppression sometimes inadvertently create further cycles of domination. For example, the Sandinista struggle against US imperialism during the 1980s inadvertently exacerbated tensions with Miskitu Indians on the East Coast of Nicuargua, leading to civil war. Likewise, Miskitu struggles against the Sandinista government produced a leadership that oppressed their own communities by terrorising those that were deemed co-opted.[143]

Many current violent struggles the world over are not only caught in this victim-offender dynamic but also alternate roles between generations. For example, prior to the Rwandan genocide, Belgian rule had set up a system of domination whereby the minority Tutsi group ruled over Hutus. After

---

[142] For more information about the genesis, growth, breakdowns, and disintegration of civilisations see Toynbee, *A Study of History.*

[143] Charles Hale, *Resistance and Contradiction: Miskitu Indians and the Nicuarguan State, 1894-1987* (Stanford: Stanford University Press, 1994).

independence, the Tutsi minority continued to hold economic and political power to the exclusion of the Hutus. In the 1990's, Hutus committed genocide against the Tutsis. Now, in the aftermath of the genocide, Tutsis are again ruling the country while hundreds of thousands of Hutus await their trials in prison, many of them dying from overcrowding and inhumane conditions.[144] Hizkias Assefa encourages us not to see Rwanda as an isolated tragedy, but rather as a mirror for humanity.[145] In one way or another we may all become caught in victim-offender cycles.

Deep-rooted victim-offender cycles and systems of domination reproduce themselves in organizations and families. For example, Israeli feminists point out that a "National Security" which wages war against Palestinians has ultimately backfired on Israeli women. Since the beginning of the first Intifada and Israel's Iron Fist policy, Israeli women have experienced an increase in rape and violence from their boyfriends, husbands, and fathers. For example Gilad Shemen, during his military service in the Occupied Territories, shot a seventeen-year-old Palestinian woman while she was on her balcony reading a book. He was not convicted of this crime and two years later, he shot and killed his nineteen-year-old Israeli ex-girlfriend.[146] Connecting violence against Palestinians to violence against Israeli women, many Palestinian and Israeli feminists have created joint organizations such as *Women Against the Occupation* and *Women in Black*.[147]

---

[144] Jean Ruremeshna, *Rwanda: Seeks to Close Overpopulated Prisons by Year-End* (Inter Press Service, April 23 2003 [cited December 14 2003]); available from http://www.afrika.no/Detailed/3398.html.

[145] Assefa, "Philosophy and Praxis of Reconciliation".

[146] Simona Sharoni, "Israel: Is Feminism a Threat to National Security?"" *Ms* (1992): 18.

[147] Hadas Lahav, "Against the Current, Women in Black" (paper presented at the Femme et Democratie au Moyen Orient, Concordia University, September 25 1993).

The fuel that keeps the system of domination running is the various roles we take (or are imposed on us) such as victim, offender, bystander, accomplice, and rescuer. Desmond Tutu explains that acting out these roles ultimately damages our humanity as well as the moral tone of the community:

> *In one way or another, as a supporter, as a perpetrator, as a victim, or one who opposed the system, something happened to our humanity, to our personhood... All South Africans were less whole than we would have been without apartheid. Those who were privileged lost out as they became more uncaring, less compassionate, less humane and therefore less human; ...those opposing apartheid frequently became brutalized themselves and descended to the same low levels as those they were opposing. The victims often ended up internalising the definition the top dogs had of them. They began to wonder whether they might not perhaps be somehow as their masters and mistresses defined them. Thus they would frequently accept that the values of the domineering class were worth striving after. And then the awful demons of self-hate and self-contempt, a hugely negative self-image, took its place in the centre of the victim's being, so corrosive of proper self-love and proper self-assurance, eating away at the very vitals of the victim's being... Society has conspired to fill you with self-hate, which you then project outward. You hate yourself and destroy yourself by proxy when you destroy those who are like this self you have been conditioned to hate.*[148]

At the heart of each role lies a common feeling of powerlessness, betrayed innocence, and self-righteousness. In fact,

---

[148] Tutu, *No Future without Forgiveness*, 196-7.

most people fall into one or more of these roles at various times in their lives or may take on several different roles within the same day or even the same relationship. For example, a person may feel victimized at work by their boss (victim), verbally attack their child (offender), and ignore a woman being beaten on the street (bystander). In this way, victims who have not had a chance to process, creatively channel, or heal their rage and hurt, can easily become offenders, accomplices, or bystanders in other situations or sometimes even within the same relationship. Gary Harper explains that victims who decide to rescue or become heroes can also easily slip into an offender role using their rage to achieve justice but in the end can hurt or control others.[149]

For example, refugees who fled Liberia to escape president Charles Taylor's authoritarian rule formed an insurgency group called Liberians United for Reconciliation and Democracy (LURD). In the process of working to overthrow president Charles Taylor they have created their own "reign of terror," killing and taking hostage thousands of innocent rural Liberians.[150] It follows that successfully transitioning from systems of domination to relationships of mutuality requires transcending these roles by nurturing a new sense of internal power, self-responsibility, and openness that can eventually foster mutual understanding and even compassion.

Embedded within every culture are teachings or roadmaps to transcend the victim-offender cycle. Peace-building and reconciliation literature tends to focus on the following five strategies: justice; education; healing and rehabilitation; narratives; political, economic, and institutional solutions.

---

[149] Gary Harper, "The Joy of Conflict Resolution: Transforming Victims, Villains and Heroes in the Workplace and at Home." Gabriola Island: New Society Publishers, 2004.

[150] Paul Welsh, *Profile: Liberia's Rebels* (2003 [cited November 18 2003]); available from http://news.bbc.co.uk/2/hi/africa/2979586.stm.

2.i. Justice

Within every culture there are teachings about how best to maintain or establish a just social order and protect human dignity.[151] For example, many of the central characteristics of our current international system had their initial articulation in the 1648 Treaty of Westphalia which is rooted in a Western political and legal culture that believes "the Nation-State and human rights is the universal foundation for social order."[152] It follows that from this perspective reconciliation requires the establishment of the rule of law and democracy. Most Nation-State approaches to reconciliation are state and human-centered, emphasizing the sovereignty of the Nation-State and the rights of the individual. For example, the international community tends to first seek to establish Western liberal visions of the rule of law and strengthen democratic institutions.[153]

In contrast, Taiaiake Alfred explains that many Indigenous notions of maintaining a just social order are "best characterized as the achievement of respectful coexistence-restoration of harmony to the network of relationships, and renewed commitment to ensuring the integrity and physical, emotional, and spiritual health of all individuals and communities."[154] In addition to re-establishing peaceful relations with oneself and with others, Indigenous notions of justice also include restoring harmonious relations with the Creator and all of creation.[155] David Abram explains that shamans in some parts of rural Asia attend to conflicts and violence within the

---

[151] Raimon Panikkar, "Is the Notion of Human Rights a Western Concept?," *Inter Culture*, no. 143 (2002): 44.

[152] Vachon, "Beyond the Religion of Human Rights, the Nation State, and the Rule of Law," 4.

[153] Laura Stovel, "Unpublished Paper Reconciliation and Restorative Justice after Mass Atrocity: Clarifying Key Concepts" (rough draft chapter in phD thesis, Simon Fraser University, 2002), 43-44.

[154] Alfred, *Peace, Power, and Righteousness: an indigenous manifesto*, 42.

[155] Ibid.

human community by working to balance its relationship to the environment. Mental illness, domestic violence, and conflict are seen as symptoms of a disharmony between nature and humans. The shaman will assess whether the human population has taken too much from the Earth and work to restore the imbalance.[156]

Clearly, notions of justice are culturally specific. Given our international system finds many of its characteristics in the Treaty of Westphalia, Western notions of justice tend to dominate transitions towards reconciliation. However, within the international community, there is a growing trend to move away from punitive justice to restorative justice.[157] Turning to restorative measures to address wrong-doing is seen as an effective way to break the never-ending victim-offender cycle as it gives an opportunity for victims to heal, perpetrators to become accountable for their actions, and to reintegrate both victims and offenders back into their communities.[158]

Frequently countries making transitions from civil war, dictatorships, or other systems of domination use both retributive and restorative measures; however, they all tend to be rooted in either a Western or Christian worldview. Special Courts and Tribunals are used to prosecute crimes against humanity as this is seen as a way to re-establish the rule of law and punish those most responsible for atrocities. Truth and reconciliation commissions are used to establish a joint truth (or narrative), come to terms with the past, offer a vehicle for victims to begin a healing process, and offenders (of lesser crimes) to take responsibility for their actions.[159] There is much debate in the field about whether this trend is useful

---

[156] David Abram, *The Spell of the Sensuous* (New York: Vintage Books, 1996), 7.

[157] Gerry Johnstone, *Restorative Justice: Ideas, Values, Debates* (Cullompton: Willan Publishing, 2002), ix

[158] Ibid., 2, Laura Stovel, "Unpublished Paper Resotorative Justice in Post-War Contexts" (Simon Fraser University, 2002), 2.

[159] Barkan, *The Guilt of Nations: Restitution and Negotiating Historical Injustices*, xxxviii; Hayner, *Unspeakable Truths*, 14.

or detrimental to the rebuilding of nations. At the heart of this debate is a tension between truth and justice.[160] Some argue truth is the most important goal after a country has lived with secrecy, lies, and collective denial.[161] Others argue punitive justice is more important as it re-establishes the ethics of right and wrong and is the key to re-establishing civil order.[162] Howard Zehr sees retributive and restorative justice as part of a larger continuum and that both are needed. For him, the legal system sets basic human rights standards and offers an important back up system to restorative processes.[163]

For Lederach, reconciliation requires truth, mercy, justice, and peace.[164] In fact, he soon began to realize that in most deep-rooted conflicts, these virtues are actually personified in many groups. For example, one group may advocate for truth, where another is fighting for justice, a third begs for mercy, and others just want peace at any cost. Lederach now sees that it is only in bringing all these voices together and learning from each of them that relationships can move towards reconciliation. As he points out, the international community has intuitively responded in this way by the creation of truth commissions (truth), amnesty provisions (mercy), tribunals (justice), and peace commissions (peace). Rather than fighting amongst ourselves over which aspect is more important (truth, justice, mercy, or peace), he suggests we need to merely learn how best to work together and in doing so, reconciliation will naturally emerge.[165]

---

[160]Hayner, *Unspeakable Truths*, 86.

[161]Cohen, *States of Denial: Knowing About Atrocities and Suffering*, 255-66; Hayner, *Unspeakable Truths*, 30.

[162] Hayner, *Unspeakable Truths*, 86; Johnstone, *Restorative Justice: Ideas, Values, Debates*, 7.

[163] Howard Zehr, *The Little Book of Restorative Justice* (Intercourse: Good Books, 2002), 17.

[164] John Paul Lederach, *The Journey toward Reconciliation* (Waterloo: Herald Press, 1999), 61.

[165] Ibid.

Finally, reparation politics is a relatively new movement where governments themselves acknowledge their role in historical injustices and make amends to the citizens they have harmed.[166] For example, in 1988, Japanese-Canadians who had been forced into internment camps during World War II were issued a formal apology from the Canadian government as well as a $20,000 compensation package.[167] In *The Guilt of Nations*, Elzar Barkan explains "the process of restitution negotiation leads to a reconfiguration on both sides. While the perpetrators hope to purge their own history of guilt and legitimise their current position, the victims hope to benefit from a new recognition of their suffering and to enjoy certain material gains."[168] Matt James argues that this leads to an increase in civic participation and a strengthening of nations.[169]

Mary Clark argues that a culture that sees justice in a restorative way that promotes social healing, on a physical and psychological level, is more likely to create conditions for reconciliation than a culture that administers solely punitive measures.[170] Whether a culture adopts the remaining four strategies to transcend the victim-offender cycle depends on its beliefs about justice: education; healing and rehabilitation; narratives; and political, economic, institutional solutions.

---

[166] Barkan, *The Guilt of Nations: Restitution and Negotiating Historical Injustices*, xv.

[167] Matt James, "Redress Politics and Canadian Citizenship," in *Canada: The State of the Federation 1998/99: Exploring the Ties That Bind*, ed. Harvey and McIntosh Lazar, Tom (Montreal and Kingston: McGill-Queen's University Press, 1999), 2.

[168] Barkan, *The Guilt of Nations: Restitution and Negotiating Historical Injustices*, 321.

[169] Ibid., xx, James, "Redress Politics and Canadian Citizenship," 23.

[170] Clark, *In Search of Human Nature*, 362.

2.ii. Education

Vern Redekop emphasizes the importance of drawing on the reconciliation teachings of the parties themselves.[171] In this way, parties are reminded to act in alignment with their own deeply held values. In addition, teaching about conditions that foster reconciliation can help parties better understand conflict and their own capacity to be a part of the solution rather than the problem.[172]

2.iii. Healing and Rehabilitation

Some practitioners and scholars emphasize the need for healing and rehabilitation in order to end the victim-offender cycle and move towards reconciliation.[173] They examine victim-offender cycles[174] and note the various opportunities for intervention and transcending these roles and ultimately regaining the fullness of one's humanity. In conflict, everyone feels hit first.[175] When we are hit hard, strong emotions such as rage, indignation, revenge, or depression can emerge. Emotions such as these activate the limbic system in our brain, immediately transmitting an adrenal message to fight or flight.[176] Redekop explains that we need to override these initial reactions by dealing with the pain, creating a safe

---

[171] Redekop, *From Violence to Blessing: How an Understanding of Deep-Rooted Conflict Can Open Paths to Reconciliation*, 292.

[172] Ibid., 326.

[173] Barry Hart, "Transforming Conflict through Trauma Recovery Training" (paper presented at the Trauma Recovery Training: Lessons Learned, Zagreb, Croatia, July 13-15 1997), 1; Judith Herman, *Trauma and Recovery: The Aftermath of Violence-from Domestic Abuse to Political Terror* (New York: Basic Books, 1997), 242; Joseph Montville, "Justice and the Burden of History," in *Reconciliation, Justice, and Coexistence: Theory and Practice*, ed. Mohammed Abu-Nimer (Lanham: Lexington Books, 2001), 142.

[174] See Appendix II

[175] Harper, "The Joy of Conflict Resolution: Transforming Victims, Villains and Heroes in the Workplace and at Home."

[176] Redekop, *From Violence to Blessing: How an Understanding of Deep-Rooted Conflict Can Open Paths to Reconciliation*, 288-91.

space, and breaking the trance[177] by humanizing the enemy image of the other, and recall reconciliation teachings.[178]

Vamik Volkan has coined the terms "chosen glory" and "chosen traumas" to explain how collective traumas are inadvertently passed down through the generations. He points out that what one group sees as their "chosen glory" is often another group's "chosen trauma." Until traumas are fully grieved they are passed down from one generation to the next.[179] Rupert Ross explains, "abuse gets passed from generation to generation, multiplying as it goes, until entire communities become engulfed by it."[180]

Again, within every culture there are tools and capacities to foster healing and rehabilitation. For example, Western practitioners, such as Judith Herman emphasize the importance of re-telling one's trauma story for the healing process.[181] Indigenous people in Canada describe seven different ways for healing to take place: "crying, yelling, talking, sweating, singing, dancing, and praying."[182] One Indigenous tool, the sweatlodge, draws on three healing activities: sweating, singing, and praying.[183]

Herman, Ross, and Clark explain that trauma can shake the very meaning we give life. Consequently, reconnection to oneself, others, and a significant meaning-making system is essential. Some studies demonstrate that healing strategies are best when they are rooted in the traditions of the victims themselves. For example, exporting Western psychotherapy

---

[177] Redekop refers to "breaking the trance" to mean being numb with fear of the other or a "dazed or stunned condition." See p.291 in Ibid.

[178] Redekop, *From Violence to Blessing: How an Understanding of Deep-Rooted Conflict Can Open Paths to Reconciliation*, 290-92.

[179] Volkan, *Blood Lines: From Ethnic Pride to Ethnic Terrorism*, 43.

[180] Ross, *Returning to the Teachings: Exploring Aboriginal Justice*, 290-92.

[181] Herman, *Trauma and Recovery: The Aftermath of Violence-from Domestic Abuse to Political Terror*, 175.

[182] Ross, *Returning to the Teachings: Exploring Aboriginal Justice*, 136.

[183] Ibid.

in some contexts may inadvertently result in a further disconnection from victims' worldviews and communities by
increasing notions of individualism and usurping the role of
local elders and healers.[184]

Though rarely written about, Mary Clark explains that
love is the best antidote for trauma. Recent brain research
shows that "stress, particularly severe and prolonged stress,
has widespread impacts on brain structure and function."[185]
Clark explains that experiencing love through "nurturing
acceptance and guidance towards autonomous development,
has the reverse effects on the brain" and is critical in the healing of social memory and trauma.[186] Developing positive
social relationships not only reduces stress, but also improves
body chemistry, which in turn benefits the body's immune
system helping it resist illnesses and overcome depression.[187]

Finally, Jung's concept of the *Shadow* is useful in understanding the creation of enemy images and how to best
humanize them.[188] Our *Shadow* is the unaccepted parts of ourselves that we tend to repress, to avoid feeling we are
"bad."[189] In fact, in repressing our *Shadow* we create dualistic
notions of good and bad, projecting what is unacceptable and
"bad" in us onto "our enemies."[190] Borris emphasizes the
importance of embracing our *Shadow* and "the totality of who
we are" in the transformation of enemy perceptions we hold

---

[184] Doe, "A View from West Africa"; Margaret Feehan, "Stories of Healing
from Native Indian Residential School Abuse" (University of Victoria, 1996);
Honwana, Edward and Green, Alcinda, *Indigenous Healing of War Affected Children in Africa* (No. 10, July 1999 [cited July 10, 2003]); available from
http://www.africaaction.org/docs99/viol9907.htm.

[185] Clark, *In Search of Human Nature*, 221.

[186] Ibid.

[187] Ibid., 226.

[188] Eileen Borris, "The Healing Power of Forgiveness," *Institute for Multi-Track
Diplomacy, occassional paper #10* 2003, 6.

[189] Ibid.

[190] Ibid.

of others."[191] For example, a francophone Quebecois man talked about how he felt animosity towards the Mohawk people for years until he realized they reminded him of his own nationalist aspirations for Quebec. Once he was able to accept his own *Shadow* and heal his own pain, he was able to join Indigenous struggles for self-determination as he recognized that their liberation is intrinsically connected to his own.[192]

Outside of punishment, restitution,[193] and restorative justice[194] there is a gap in reconciliation literature on the rehabilitation of offenders. South Africa's experience demonstrates that this is an area in desperate need of attention. Granting amnesty to perpetrators was a politically negotiated necessity for the smooth transition from apartheid to democracy; however Mary Clark explains that the consequences are only now being felt as secondary violence within Black communities skyrockets.[195] Similarly, there is relatively little written about the role of bystanders, accomplices, or rescuers. Stanley Cohen's book *Denial in the Face of Atrocities* outlines the role of denial in the maintenance of these roles and suggests ways to move parties towards truth telling and accountability.[196] Clearly, there is a need for more grounded theory on the rehabilitation of offenders as many grassroots initiatives such as the reintegration of soldiers in Mozambique and various Indigenous justice initiatives in Canada are far more common than existing

---

[191] Ibid., 6-7.

[192] anonymous, personal communication, August 5, 2002.

[193] Barkan, *The Guilt of Nations: Restitution and Negotiating Historical Injustices.*

[194] For a comprehensive summary of restorative justice literature and postwar reconciliation see Stovel, "Unpublished Paper Restorative Justice in Post-War Contexts".

[195] Clark, *In Search of Human Nature*, 363.

[196] Cohen, *States of Denial: Knowing About Atrocities and Suffering*, 6-160.

reconciliation and peace-building documentation demon-strates.[197]

2.iv. Narratives

Volkan explains that healing work needs to accompany a re-storying of narratives. In creating joint narratives parties no longer pass down hate and prejudice through the genera-tions, factual consensus is created, and moral standards are established. For example, while the South African Truth and Reconciliation Commission had several pitfalls, a national narrative was created that confirmed apartheid and its crimes were wrong, thereby creating a new moral standard for South Africa.[198] At their best, truth commissions can be important fact-finding bodies that produce "a sophisticated historical account of a violent past which integrates a structural analy-sis with the consciousness of those who lived through it." [199]

John Winslade and Gerald Monk argue that conflict is not motivated from within people's psyches but rather emerges "from people's shared social and cultural fabric."[200] For example, a fight between Maori and white students in a small rural community in New Zealand merely reflects "the much larger historical and contemporary traditional adversaries"

---

[197] Kelly MacDonald, "Literature Review: Implications of Restorative Justice in Cases of Violence against Aboriginal Women and Children," (Vancouver: Aboriginal Women's Action Network, 2001); Ross, *Returning to the Teachings: Exploring Aboriginal Justice,* Audrey Huntley, Wendy Stewart, and Fay Blaney, "The Implications of Restorative Justice for Aboriginal Women and Children Survivors of Violence: A Comparative Overview of Five Communities in British Columbia," (Vancouver: Aboriginal Women's Action Network, 2001).

[198] Hayner, *Unspeakable Truths*, 160.

[199] Richard A Wilson, *The Politics of Truth and Reconciliation in South Africa: Legitimizing the Post-Apartheid State* (Cambridge: Cambridge University Press, 2001), 228.

[200] Winslade, John and Monk, Gerald, "Finding Common Ground between Traditional Adversaries: A Narrative Approach in Mediation" (paper pre-sented at the American Anthropology Conference, New Orleans, November 2002), 1.

within the larger society.[201] Their narrative approach to mediation involves including the story of the larger society as well as the individuals involved. They explain that stories are how people make meaning and hence working with parties' stories can lead to on-going dialogue and relationships of mutuality rather than merely coming to agreements where the conversation ends.[202]

One aspect that is frequently overlooked in the literature concerning narratives and reconciliation is the importance to not only establish factual truth but also worldview truth. When a group's code of ethics is violated, feelings of deep indignation and victimhood fester. For example, Leroy Little Bear explains that his people (Blackfoot) invited early settlers to ceremonies as a way to introduce the newcomers to their ways of taking care of the land. As a gesture of brotherhood, the Blackfoot gave sacred objects used in the ceremonies to the settlers, symbolizing their new joint effort to take care of the land. From the settler perspective, they assumed Indigenous people would not last as distinct cultures and collected these objects to sell to museums.[203] These vastly different worldviews linked to notions of ethics and justice are often the beginning of on-going victim-offender dynamics and need to be central to the development of narratives for fostering reconciliation.

2.v. Political, Economic, and Institutional Solutions

Still others point to the importance of political and economic solutions that address everyone's basic human needs.[204] For example, Hizkias Assefa argues that the world currently

---

[201] Ibid., 2.

[202] Ibid., 3-4.

[203] Loretta Todd, "Kainayssini Imanistaisiwa: The People Go On," ed. Loretta Todd (Toronto: National Film Board, 2003).

[204] Clark, *In Search of Human Nature*, 404, Redekop, *From Violence to Blessing: How an Understanding of Deep-Rooted Conflict Can Open Paths to Reconciliation*, 301.

needs a massive redistribution of resources in order to bring peace to many regions in the world.[205] Mary Clark echoes his words and explains real peace must start with economic justice.[206] Many critics of the South African Truth and Reconciliation Commission point to the lack of economic justice. They argue a black face may have been put on South African politics, however the purse strings remain in the control of the white minority.[207] Assefa likens South Africa's economic apartheid to the current global apartheid where northern countries reap the benefit of the majority of the world's resources.[208]

Redekop argues that human beings have the following five fundamental identity needs: meaning, connectedness, security, recognition, and action/autonomy.[209] Structures that deny these fundamental human identity needs, he claims, foster violence. It follows that structural change, which ensures the basic human needs of everyone, is essential for reconciliation to be possible.

Perhaps justice, education, healing and rehabilitation, narratives, political, economic, and institutional solutions all contribute to creating conditions for reconciliation. Particular strategies, however, are only valuable if they are able to transcend victim-offender cycles, strengthen cultural consistency, and foster cultures of peace. In doing so, parties are able to begin to regain the fullness of their humanity and re-establish (or establish for the first time) principled communities.

---

[205] Assefa, "Philosophy and Praxis of Reconciliation", Barkan, *The Guilt of Nations: Restitution and Negotiating Historical Injustices*, xi.

[206] Clark, *In Search of Human Nature*, 361.

[207] Assefa, "Philosophy and Praxis of Reconciliation".

[208] Ibid.

[209] Redekop, *From Violence to Blessing: How an Understanding of Deep-Rooted Conflict Can Open Paths to Reconciliation*, 31.

3. Large-Scale Social Change

The heart of reconciliation is fundamentally a large-scale social change
process from the inside out. Transitioning from systems of domination to
relationships of mutuality requires a
parallel process of personal and societal
change. Neglecting to attend to one's inner
terrain[210] can inadvertently add fuel to already
volatile conflicts rather than bring peace. For
example, in our haste to bring order to chaos, many international peace-building initiatives often impose Western solutions that further erode local culture and hence inadvertently
dismantle local capacities.[211] Similarly, using force to "fix"
deep-rooted conflict merely intensifies victim-offender cycles
as can be seen in the current U.S intervention in Iraq.

Despite the fact that the majority of contemporary deep-
rooted conflicts have shifted from between states to within
nations themselves, traditional top-down approaches to reconciliation and peace remain the predominant approach. The
challenges facing the top-down model include outmoded
ideas of representation, an inability to implement agreements, and the difficulty of high visibility in the making of
peace accords.[212]

Representation is no longer clear in most conflicts as fewer
people feel truly represented by their leaders. Moreover,
power is much more diffuse with the increase in non-governmental organizations, factions, corporations, interest groups,
and organized groups willing to use political violence to

---

[210] Michelle LeBaron uses this term to refer to learning about one's cultural
autobiography and understanding how early experiences shape who we are,
what we see, and how we respond. LeBaron, *Bridging Cultural Conflicts: A New
Approach for a Changing World*, 87.

[211] Doe, "A View from West Africa," 160.

[212] Lederach, "Fundamentals of Peace-Building".

achieve their goals.[213] As a result, top down negotiated peace accords can lead to a precarious "peace" as corrupt governments broker agreements with violent guerrilla groups, and non-violent grassroots organizations are left out of the discussion altogether. For example, recently the Ivory Coast government, with the assistance of France, brokered a peace accord with the main rebel group. All three parties have significant interests in power and resources and have all used coercive means to attain their goals. This peace deal was rejected by the people and continues to be riddled with difficulty.[214]

The second significant challenge to the top-down approach is that this model assumes a hierarchy of power. In essence, can the people at the table in this process deliver what they agree to? Power is not so neat and cleanly distributed. As mentioned above, power is diffuse. People who are not included in a process will become pockets of resistance. Similarly, a government alone cannot change the consciousness of a country. For example, in 1993 Israeli Prime Minister Yitzhak Rabin and Palestinian Liberation Organization leader Yasser Arafat signed the Oslo Accord, which outlined a peace agreement. Neither Israeli nor Palestinian grassroots were involved so the daily violence between the two did not lead to lasting peace, and ultimately the peace accord failed. Clearly, this model of diplomacy does not help with present-day realities.[215]

The third challenge with top leadership negotiations is that the negotiations are highly visible, which creates a dilemma for parties around openness towards concessions and transparency. Highly visible leaders tend to speak in a way that shows their strength because concessions are perceived by their own people as co-optation. The desire to be seen as strong in the short term can easily become more

---

[213] Ibid.

[214] West African Network for Education and Peace, *Crisis in Cote D'ivoire* (Fewer, 2003 [cited January 5 2004]); available from www.fewer.org.

[215] Lederach, "Fundamentals of Peace-Building".

important than a fair and lasting agreement. The challenge becomes how to open space for creativity and concessions as well as maintain a level of public transparency. This becomes especially difficult when leaders risk their lives if they attempt to move their people in a new direction. Montville argues a space needs to be created to explore ideas before they become public. For example, during the Oslo Accords, top leadership met privately to allow for movement in a new direction. However, when parties eventually came to an agreement and went public, it was seen as a lack of consultation.[216] Tragically, Israeli Prime Minister Yitzhak Rabin was later murdered by more extreme elements within Israeli society.

Lederach explains that having a purely grassroots approach to peace-building can increase the consciousness of a group but often fails to bring about structural change.[217] For example, drawing from the Australian experience, National Sorry Day has been an effective grassroots movement that transformed the consciousness of many Australians. As a result, one million people marched apologizing to Aboriginal people for "the Stolen Generation," when government officials forcibly removed Aboriginal children from their families and placed them in residential schools. In addition, dialogue groups, educational modules, and traditional storytelling were developed and implemented to build relationships and raise consciousness. Despite a dramatic increase in grassroots awareness and commitment to righting relationships with Aboriginal people, the Australian state refuses to acknowledge its responsibility for its role in colonialism or "The Stolen Generation." As a result, little or no real structural change has been achieved. Indeed many issues with regards to land, governance, and human rights remain neglected. Furthermore, ordinary Australians have been apologizing for

---

[216] Ibid.

[217] Ibid.

several years, and the grassroots enthusiasm at times loses its momentum.[218]

In light of the difficulties of unilateral top down or grass-roots peace processes, Lederach argues that effective reconciliation processes must engage grassroots, middle, and top government leadership. In this way, transitions from systems of domination to relationships of mutuality involve shifting from a top down approach to developing and strengthening multi-level networks to engage in a large-scale social change process.[219]

Lederach likens this approach to a spider weaving its web. In this way, reconciliation initiatives need to endeavour to build strategic alliances with unlike minded people and unlike situated people. Regardless of our position in society (top, middle, or grassroots), our tendency is to build alliances with people who are like-minded and like-situated. Lederach, insists we must be more strategic in our alliance building and weave webs or relationships like spiders. These insects choose three or four anchors and weave various levels together. Likewise, he suggests that peacebuilders need to consider two essential questions:

1. In this context who has trust and relationships in all levels of leaderships (grassroots, middle, and top)? This question is essentially about **vertical capacity**: what people, institutions, organisations have the capacity to effect change? Who has the capacity to cross the invisible line of division to have relationships with their own group and the other groups?

2. What are the collective social divisions (geographic, linguistic, familial, political)? What organizations,

---

[218] Huggins, Jackie. First Nations Reconciliation Conference 2002, Vancouver. It is only through the perseverance and the strategic alliance building that we are beginning to see some changes. See p.123-124 of this book for an example of an upcoming public memorial.

[219] Lederach, "Fundamentals of Peace-Building".

people, and institutions have **horizontal capacities**? Who has horizontal capacity that can cut across horizontal divisions?

In this way the key is to pay attention to where people are located and think about how best to create relationships horizontally and vertically. Within deep-rooted conflict this is more difficult than it appears. People who are able to build relationships across difference are often seen as either co-opted sell-outs or spies, making this work especially difficult and even dangerous in some contexts.[220]

I would broaden Lederach's approach to suggest the importance of developing one's own worldviewing skills as well as capacities to transcend the victim-offender cycle. We are all part and parcel of systems of domination and have to greater or lesser degrees internalised worldview dominance or subjugation. Moreover, we all have taken on roles such as victim, offender, bystander, accomplice or rescuer. In developing our own skills first we can avoid one of the biggest obstacles facing social change movements – internal "territoriality, jealousy, and competition."[221] Being attuned to one's own worldview and that of others is essential in order to avoid social change strategies that inadvertently erode culture. For example, a peacebuilder may assume the elected representative is a community's most valued leader; however it may actually be elders, clan mothers, or teachers. In working solely with an elected leader, local capacities for peace and good governance may inadvertently be undermined. Moreover, in transcending our own internalised victim-offender roles, social change agents are better able to model how to transcend this dynamic and avoid colluding with others caught up in the cycle.

---

[220] Ibid.

[221] John Paul Lederach, "Frontier Luncheon" (paper presented at the Eastern Mennonite University Summer Peace-building Institute, Harrisonburg, May 22 2002).

Reconciliation "from the inside out" involves putting one's own house in order and strategizing from whatever place we may find ourselves in the web of relationships. For example, an academic may begin to incorporate worldviewing skills and perspectives on whatever topic she may be teaching. Similarly, the director of a government agency will recognize his own position in the victim-offender cycle and begin to fund programs that foster worldviewing skills as well as capacities to transcend the victim-offender cycle. What is essential is that each person starts with who they are and where they are, and weave webs of relationships from that position.

4. Timing and Tactics

Effective social change starts with where things are rather than where we would like them to be.[222] In deep-rooted conflicts, there can be a tendency to enter negotiations and reach settlements before assessing what stage the conflict is in and what would be the best strategies and activities to attain sustainable peace and reconciliation. There is a variety of conflict mapping,[223] early warning risk assessment,[224] and reconciliation cycle awareness tools.[225] While it is beyond the scope of this book to summarize all of them, I will briefly touch on some aspects of timing and tactics related to developing worldviewing skills, transcending the victim-offender

---

[222] Alinsky, *Rules for Radicals: A Pragmatic Primer for Realistic Radicals*, 185.

[223] Lederach, *Building Peace: Sustainable Reconciliation in Divided Societies*, 70.

[224] See *Early Warning Risk Assessment* ([cited November 15th 2003]); available from www.fewer.org.

[225] Larry Dunn, "The Process of Forgiveness-an Excercise," *MCS Conciliation Quarterly* (1995): 31.

dynamic, and building a large-scale social change movement for reconciliation.

4.i Assess Relationships of Mutuality
a. Assess Worldviewing Skills

Given that culture is closely linked to our identity and how we make meaning in the world it is essential to assess the cultural fluency of the parties involved. Is there a dominant cultural lens that is used to name, frame, and tame[226] the conflict? Is this part of a larger history of colonial or imperial domination? If so, how can we develop more sophisticated worldviewing skills on all sides so that we can engage in culturally relevant dispute handling processes? Moreover, how can we regenerate cultures that have been eroded or distorted in this context?

b. Assess Victim-Offender Cycle
Level of Denial

Denial is the glue that keeps systems of domination in place. Groups living within systems of domination typically produce inaccurate narratives to protect themselves from the truth and avoid change. Typically the "dominant" group denies the unjust relationship, avoids accountability, and sees the conflict only from their narrow viewpoint or worldview. Similarly, "victim" groups tend to internalise the messages from the dominant group and may also deny the extent of the unjust relationship and/or actively participate in it. Alternatively, the "victim" group may conflate historical fact and create a "victim" narrative that only serves in the long run to further disempower their group and avoid addressing the heart of the matter. It is therefore crucial to assess the level of denial in any deep-rooted conflict.

---

[226] Michelle LeBaron refers to the terms "name, frame and tame" conflicts in LeBaron, *Bridging Cultural Conflicts: A New Approach for a Changing World*, 12.

Level of Trauma

In many deep-rooted conflicts, the "victim group" typically responds in two ways. One, by internalising abuse and continuing a legacy of intergenerational trauma, high suicide rates, addictions, high crime rates, unemployment, despair, hopelessness, factionalism, increased violence against women and children, and abuse of power by local leadership. Two, by externalising the violence and joining rebel and guerrilla organizations. Both reactions are a result of trauma; one kills themselves, while the second kills others.

While this may not be immediately apparent, "dominant" or "offender" groups tend to have a level of trauma as well. Desmond Tutu explains that in participating and benefiting from an unjust system, offenders lose important aspects of their own humanity such as compassion, openness, generosity, and honesty.[227] Furthermore, most, if not all, "offender groups" have an earlier history (sometimes hundreds of years ago) of being the victim group. They also carry the intergenerational trauma associated with that earlier victimization. Moreover, within their own group they tend to have their own victim-offender dynamics such as violence against women or other minority groups. This history in no way justifies their actions, however it can be helpful in understanding and and determining appropriate strategies.

Some initial questions to assess a victim-offender cycle include: Who are the groups involved in a victim-offender cycle? And what is the impact on each group? What is the level of trauma? What are the surface trauma needs? What are the structural issues currently contributing to trauma that need to be addressed?

c. Assess the level of participation

There is a close relationship between the engaged participation of all sectors of society in a peace process and its

---

[227] Tutu, *No Future without Forgiveness*, 196-97.

success in fostering large-scale social change. The closer people feel to the process of change, the more they will have ownership and therefore greater trust will be built between parties and the process.[228] Many reconciliation processes tend to exclude the more radical elements of a conflict. Experience shows us that inclusiveness, no matter how uncomfortable, is key to fostering reconciliation.[229] In this way, assessing the level of participation in efforts to resolve conflicts between groups is essential. Are the processes generally amongst top leadership or do they involve all sectors of society? Are all perspectives represented in peace processes? Who is excluded and why? What do we need to do to broaden participation?

4.ii. Current Capacities and Commitment/Good Will

Creating conditions for lasting reconciliation requires resources, capacity, as well as whole-hearted commitment and good will. Here are some beginning questions to ask:

a. Assess Capacity

What are the current human resources for fostering reconciliation: who are the healers, teachers, and elders? What are the financial resources? What is the local knowledge pertaining to reconciliation? Is governance rooted in local culture? What is the current level of integrity or corruption?

b. Assess Commitment/Good Will

Assessing the commitment and good will of the parties involved goes beyond words and financial contributions. In fact, great words and expensive dispute resolution processes can be part of a larger avoidance pattern and give the illusion of change yet maintain the status quo. The presence of any of the following six red flags may indicate a lack of commitment and good will: incongruence between language and actions, pseudo-apologies, a focus on individual settlement rather than

---

[228] Lederach, "Fundamentals of Peace-Building".

[229] Ibid.

large-scale social change, commissions and reports that are promptly shelved, questionable dispute resolution processes that either protect perpetrators or seek revenge, and exclusion.[230]

Assessing relationships of mutuality (level of denial, trauma, worldviewing skills, and participation), capacity, and good will merely adds a further dimension to pre-existing conflict assessment tools. For example, if the conflict is characterized by worldview domination, strategies would focus on developing worldviewing skills amongst parties. Similarly, for parties caught in the throes of victim-offender cycles, strategies would include exposing the truth, healing, and rehabilitation. Moreover, time may need to be taken to assess the capacities and good will of the parties themselves. For example, if there is a high level of trauma and few healing resources exist, strategies must include developing these capacities.

As worldviewing skills and capacities to transcend victim-offender cycles are learned and relationships become more balanced, parties begin to move into more authentic relationships. This authenticity could include an increase in openness and confrontation as real issues are put on the table. Only once relationships are characterized by mutuality, a fuller picture is established, and adequate capacities are available can parties begin genuine negotiation. Bypassing these stages can result in negotiations between parties that are either marked by collective denial, trauma, or both, resulting in a continuation of the victim-offender cycle rather than a transformation of systems of domination.[231] While many conflict assessment models are portrayed as linear sequential frameworks, in reality conflict assessment is less clear-cut, because relationships are constantly evolving, often in unpredictable ways. The ques-

---

[230] An exploration of each of these 'red flags' is beyond the scope of this chapter; however various elements are described throughout this book.

[231] For an example of how survivors of residential school survivors have been re-victimized in settlement negotiations in Canada see Hodgson, "Residential School: 'A Shared Journey' in Redefining Relationships," 26-27.

tions I have put forward offer a new lens to begin to discern effective strategies to create conditions to foster reconciliation.

In summary, the four guiding touchstones can be seen both as starting points as well as places to return for reflexive reconciliation praxis. Clearly reconciliation is a complex praxis and has several dimensions. One of the most pernicious aspects of deep-rooted conflict is the imposition of one worldview on another. This aspect, however, is often neglected in the literature.

Bringing worldviews into full awareness, *Part Two* weaves metaphors, storytelling, legends and theory together to illustrate worldviewing skills and the capacities needed to create conditions ripe for reconciliation, bridge cultural differences, and rekindle global worldview pluralism.

Chapter Two, *The Singing Mediator,* illustrates the importance of connecting parties to their fundamental worldviews as a way to strengthen personal integrity, cultural consistency, and local capacity, consequently creating conditions for meaningful and lasting reconciliation. In this way, a practitioner not only assists in resolving disputes, but helps foster lasting cultures of peace.

Chapter Three, *When Worlds Collide,* builds on the skills of the first chapter and demonstrates the difficulties when conflicting parties have fundamentally different worldviews and the necessity to develop ways to engage across worldview difference, deepen our own cultural roots, broaden our understanding about life, and lay the relational foundation to address difficult substantive issues.

Chapter Four, *Out of the Ashes, Phoenix Rises* adds to the skills and knowledge learned in the previous two chapters and addresses one of the most difficult challenges facing the world today: rekindling worldview pluralism through the regeneration of Indigenous cultures and the re-civilising of the Western cultures.

Finally, in Part Three, *The Way Out,* I conclude with *The Stone in Your Shoe* which simultaneously connects worldviewing skills to the bigger picture as well as lays out the personal work necessary for a parallel process of personal and political transformation.

PART TWO

Worldviewing Skills

CHAPTER 2

THE SINGING MEDIATOR

In the 1980s, Burkina Faso and Mali went to war over the border. Several conferences and mediation efforts were made to end the conflict, but none succeeded in convincing the parties to pursue peace. The President of Guinea at that time, Ahmed Sekou Touré, invited Presidents Thomas Sankara and Moussa Traoré of Burkina Faso and Mali, respectively. In front of the presidential palace in Conakry, one of West Africa's celebrated griots (praise singer), Kanja Kouyate, put on a spectacular performance before the host and visiting presidents. The performance took on the form of entertainment, but Kanja Kouyate was calling on the two presidents at war to make peace. He did this by evoking their ancestors and appealing to their inherent human goodness as leaders to lead their people out of conflict. Through poetry, song, and dance, he brought out qualities that were a hallmark

of a true African leader and challenged the two presidents to look to their ancestors and bring back dignity instead of shame and suffering to their peoples. So emotional was this performance that the two presidents not only shed tears and embraced publicly, but took a solemn oath before the public and witnessed by their ancestors not to return to war. On their return home, they called an urgent meeting and signed a peace agreement that has never been violated since then. Not only did the war end, but also cooperative relations between the two countries have increased dramatically as well.[232]

This story illustrates that connecting conflicting parties to the bigger picture, or their worldview, is the best way to create conditions ripe for reconciliation. Embedded in every culture and tradition are teachings that foster right action, peaceful coexistence, and reconciliation.[233] Tapping into those teachings, whether they are secular, humanistic values or spiritually based insights, inspires parties to live in alignment with their highest ideals. Rather than respond from a place of victimhood, parties can override the desire to hit back, or be right at all costs, and discover an internal power based on personal integrity and right action.[234]

Within every culture there are teachings and traditions "designed to help people get along with one another."[235] Redekop defines teachings as "the customs, moral imperatives, and stories that together develop a moral outlook that enables one to make good decisions while walking the path

---

[232] Excerpted from Doe, "A View from West Africa," 164.

[233] Assefa, "Peace and Reconciliation as a Paradigm: A Philosophy of Peace and Its Implications on Conflict, Governance and Economic Growth," 9; Redekop, *From Violence to Blessing: How an Understanding of Deep-Rooted Conflict Can Open Paths to Reconciliation*, 292.

[234] Parry, *Warriors of the Heart*, 35.

[235] Redekop, *From Violence to Blessing: How an Understanding of Deep-Rooted Conflict Can Open Paths to Reconciliation*, 292.

of life. It defines what is central and most important with the idea that one not stray too far to the right or to the left."[236] For example, during South Africa's transition from apartheid, Archbishop Desmond Tutu drew on the African notion of *ubuntu*, which speaks to the very essence of being human, that is "my humanity is caught up, inextricably bound up in yours. We belong in a bundle of life."[237] Drawing on *ubuntu* as a concept and a teaching, Tutu lay the foundation for reconciliation between perpetrators and victims.

In a similar vein, Mahatma Gandhi's successful campaign for self-rule in India was based on a spiritual insight that there is "many sidedness of truth...(and that) religions are different roads converging to the same point."[238] Gandhi found that the principle of *ahimsa* or non-violence was embedded in Jain, Buddhist, Hindu, and Christian teachings. Consequently, basing the political struggle for self-rule on the principle of *ahimsa*, he worked to unite the various religions within India for the same goal. For Gandhi, the means and ends are akin to a seed and a tree – "we reap exactly what we sow."[239] It follows, he argued, non-violent action to achieve self-rule was the only way to achieve a sovereign and peaceful India.[240] Drawing on a composite of two Hindi words, *satyagraha*, Gandhi described a non-violent strategy that relies on exposing the truth (*satya*) and holding firmly (*graha*).[241] He believed that one must start with the consciousness of the individual to build a strong non-violent movement. As Indians understood their own cooperation with their oppression, they would more easily engage in non-

---

[236] Ibid.

[237] Tutu, *No Future without Forgiveness*, 31.

[238] Correspondence from Rajchandra Ravjibhai Mehta to Gandhi in Peter; Duval Ackerman, Jack, *A Force More Powerful: A Century of Nonviolent Conflict* (New York: Palgrave, 2000), 64.

[239] Ibid., 65.

[240] Ibid.

[241] Ibid.

cooperation with the British. In turn, breaking laws and exposing the truth of the injustices imposed on Indians, Gandhi felt that the British themselves would eventually awaken to their own humanity and leave India on their own accord.[242] Inspired by Gandhi's success, Dr. Martin Luther King drew on the principles of *satyagraha* and *ahimsa* as well as Christian teachings to build a successful large-scale civil rights movement in the United States.[243]

Vietnamese peace activist and Buddhist monk, Thich Nhat Hanh, explains that in his tradition reconciliation can only be attained if we "first learn ways to deal peacefully with ourselves...Techniques are always secondary."[244] Becoming peace is at the heart of Buddhist tradition, so that regardless of the circumstances, one is able to respond in a way that does not create further suffering.[245] In essence, reconciliation teachings, regardless of the tradition or discipline, help people travel from hatred, greed, victim or oppressor to peaceful relations within oneself and with all of creation.

Hizkias Assefa argues that reconciliation is ultimately a paradigm shift from staunch individualism to one that fosters interdependence between humans and all of creation. He identifies four dimensions to reconciliation embedded in many traditions and cultures: reconciliation with the spiritual realm, reconciliation with one's self, reconciliation with others, and reconciliation with nature.[246] Each dimension is not a linear process, but rather a series of highly interrelated relationships, that flow one into another (see Figure 5).

---

[242] Ibid.

[243] Ibid., 308.

[244] Thich Nhat Hahn, "Ahimsa: The Path of Harmlessness," in *Buddhist Peacework*, ed. David Chappell (Boston: Wisdom Publications, 1999), 158.

[245] Ibid.

[246] Assefa, "Peace and Reconciliation as a Paradigm: A Philosophy of Peace and Its Implications on Conflict, Governance and Economic Growth," 10-13.

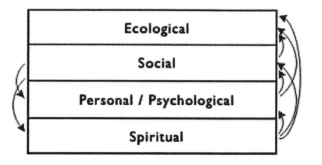

Figure 5: The Four Dimensions of Reconciliation[247]

According to Assefa the first dimension has to do with spiritual reconciliation.[248] I would venture to broaden this to suggest it is reconciliation with one's cosmology, in this way this model includes secular visions of reality. Essentially, it involves understanding our relationship to the "bigger picture"[249] and living in alignment with those teachings or values.[250] We must ask ourselves questions such as "What do I value most?" "What do I believe about creation?" "What does my family believe?" "And what do my people believe?" going as far back as one can. The exercise is not necessarily to return to these exact teachings but rather to enter into a process of deliberate worldviewing. That is we seek to rediscover, revise, and realign with a cosmology that is meaningful to each individual and which promotes peaceful co-existence. Spiritual

---

[247] Ibid., 16. Reprinted with permission from the author; see Appendix V.

[248] Ibid., 10.

[249] Michelle LeBaron's definition of spirituality in *Bridging Cultural Conflicts: A New Approach for a Changing World*, 94.

[250] Assefa, "Peace and Reconciliation as a Paradigm: A Philosophy of Peace and Its Implications on Conflict, Governance and Economic Growth," 10; Chief Robert Joseph, personal communication, August 5 2003, LeBaron, *Bridging Cultural Conflicts: A New Approach for a Changing World*, 170; Redekop, *From Violence to Blessing: How an Understanding of Deep-Rooted Conflict Can Open Paths to Reconciliation*, 292-93.

reconciliation, Assefa asserts, is an essential part of reconciliation as it reconnects or strengthens one's connection to not only the spiritual realm, but indeed to all of creation.[251] Tillich encompasses both spiritual and secular quests for meaning when he describes religion as "an ultimate concern, a concern which qualifies all other concerns as preliminary and which itself contains the answer to the question of a meaning of our life."[252]

Assefa considers reconciliation with the self the second dimension of an overall reconciliation process (see Figure 5). I might recast this as a question asking "How have I lived, and how do I live in congruency with my cosmology and code of ethics?" This requires self-reflection and honesty regardless of the tradition one is coming from. The specifics differ, however, depending on one's tradition. For Christians it would involve a request for forgiveness from God for any offences committed.[253] Hindus would assess whether they had transcended the karma they have been given.[254] For others not connected to a faith tradition, it may involve a taking stock of one's actions, making adjustments where necessary, and strengthening one's commitments and values. LeBaron refers to this as the process of taking care of one's inner terrain through alignment and attunement with one's values.[255]

The third dimension involves reconciliation with others includes reflecting on our relationships with our neighbours and the human community at large. Engaging in self-reflection and asking whether "in our relationships, are we living in alignment with our values?" This too involves honest self-

---

[251] Assefa, "Peace and Reconciliation as a Paradigm: A Philosophy of Peace and Its Implications on Conflict, Governance and Economic Growth," 10-13.

[252] Michael Suman, *Religion and Prime Time Television* (Connecticut and London: Praeger Publishers, 1997), 118.

[253] Assefa, "Peace and Reconciliation as a Paradigm: A Philosophy of Peace and Its Implications on Conflict, Governance and Economic Growth," 10.

[254] Fitmaurice, "Other Religions and Reconciliation," 173-74.

[255] LeBaron, *Bridging Cultural Conflicts: A New Approach for a Changing World*, 170.

reflection and a commitment to making changes where necessary. Assefa writes that in many traditions spiritual reconciliation is not possible until one has reconciled with one's neighbour (meaning all other human beings). For example, Muslims are required to ask for forgiveness from anyone they may have offended during their lives before being allowed to visit Mecca.[256] Similarly, during Yom Kippur, Jewish people are encouraged to make apologies to all they may have hurt during the previous year.[257] In this way one makes reparations and adjustments wherever necessary. Reconciliation with others also involves forgiveness or letting go of ways in which one has been harmed by others.[258] It calls for self-responsibility to heal what has been hurt and to develop compassionate strength – that is the ability to assert one's own needs while simultaneously developing compassion and understanding for the other.[259]

Finally, reconciliation with nature (see Figure 5) comes from an understanding that one cannot be reconciled with one's cosmology while simultaneously living in a disrespectful and abusive relationship towards the Earth and all non-human beings. Again honest self-reflection of not only our present relationship with nature, but also an exploration of the historical roots of our disconnection from the land is necessary. For many Indigenous people, this is at the heart of their traditional spiritual beliefs – living in harmony with the interdependency of the natural world.[260] Though expressed

---

[256] Assefa, "Philosophy and Praxis of Reconciliation".

[257] Marianne Williamson, *Healing the Soul of America: Reclaiming Our Voices as Spiritual Citizens* (New York: Touchstone, 1997), 89.

[258] Assefa, "Peace and Reconciliation as a Paradigm: A Philosophy of Peace and Its Implications on Conflict, Governance and Economic Growth," 11.

[259] Robert and Folger Bush, Joseph, *The Promise of Mediation* (San Francisco: Jossey Bass, 1994), 233; Linn, Dennis; Linn, Sheila; and Linn, Mathew, *Don't Forgive Too Soon, Extending the Two Hands That Heal* (New York: Paulist Press, 1997).

[260] Abram, *The Spell of the Sensuous*, 71; Alfred, *Peace, Power, and Righteousness: an indigenous manifesto*, 42, Erasmus, *Third Annual Lafontaine-Baldwin Lecture* ([cited March 16 2002]).

differently, Assefa shows how within a Christian worldview, scripture clearly outlines that in abusing God's creation one violates one's relationship with God and oneself.[261] Similarly, secular values around conserving energy, recycling, and re-using are part and parcel of mainstream Canada and public policy. Honest self-reflection requires efforts to reconnect with nature as well as working to end all human exploitation of the Earth.[262]

By integrating the individual, society and nature, reconciliation "becomes a comprehensive paradigm from which to discern life and relationships in general, instead of being simply a technique for dealing with social disputes."[263] Moreover, reconciliation fosters an interdependence that is not merely utilitarian but one that is "rooted in a notion of deep spiritual and material interconnectedness which links human beings and nature to a common foundation." [264]

Reminding parties of the fundamental values that foster reconciliation can help parties connect to their own humanity. In *Warriors Heart*, Danaan Parry explains there are three layers to all human beings: the *Persona*, the *Shadow*, and the *Self* (see Figure 6 on following page).[265] The *Persona* is what we like to show others: our position in society, successes, and credentials. The *Shadow* is right below the surface and includes all the things we don't want others to see such as our mistakes, certain emotions, and our sense of being wounded. Finally, the *Self* is the core of who we are as human beings. It is the place where we know we are whole, complete and can tap into a wellspring of love that connects us to other human beings and creation itself.[266]

---

[261] Assefa, "Peace and Reconciliation as a Paradigm: A Philosophy of Peace and Its Implications on Conflict, Governance and Economic Growth," 14.

[262] Ibid., 15.

[263] Ibid., 17.

[264] Ibid.

[265] Parry, *Warriors of the Heart*, 39.

[266] Ibid., 37-38.

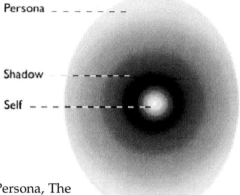

Persona

Shadow

Self

Figure 6: The Persona, The
Shadow, and the Self[267]

In conflict, people tend to respond from their persona as
well as project their shadow onto their "enemies." Within cultures, rituals[268] have been developed to assist parties to return
to *ile tempore*, or the beginning of time, as a way to dismantle
inner defences, let go of the old, and allow for the regeneration of the parties' themselves and their collectivities. Tapping into parties' creation stories "reactualizes...mythical
times in which...Divine Beings were creating or organizing
the earth."[269] In turn, creative forces are released during the
re-telling of the creation story, allowing for the mystical death
and rebirth of the parties themselves, the world, and human
society as a whole.[270]

Reconciliation teachings and regenerative rituals help parties connect to their core selves, relinquish the need to be right,
heal their shadows, and tap into an internal power based on
personal integrity and connection to the bigger picture. *The*

---

[267] Ibid. Reprinted with the permission of the publisher; see Appendix V.

[268] Chapter 5 *Out of The Ashes, Phoenix Rises* of this book gives examples of a
variety of rituals that offer death and rebirth metaphors for life's journey.

[269] Mircea Eliade, *Birth and Rebirth: The Religious Meanings of Initiation in
Human Culture* (New York: Harper & Brothers Publishers, 1958), 19.

[270] Ibid., xxii.

Singing Mediator illustrates this regenerative capacity beauti-
fully. In inviting the *griot* to do a performance, the Malian and
Burkinabé presidents were reminded of the long history of
dignified African leadership prior to colonization when *griots*
were often used as respected advisors to some of the greatest
West African kings and princes. Traditionally and still today,
griots are given their role at birth and are considered a special
caste that learn the entire oral history of their region and how
to transmit its lessons through the art of spoken word and
song. They memorize all significant events in their village
including births, deaths, marriages, hunts, seasons, and wars.
In this way, they are responsible for preserving memory, ensuring cultural consistency, and fostering community cohesion.
Through song, poetry, storytelling and dance, *griots* pass on
the richness of the culture and important lessons during significant events. For example, a *griot* may be invited to a wedding
to remind the newly-weds of their responsibilities and joys, as
well as transmit lessons about overcoming difficulties. When
griots perform, typically they speak for hours and sometimes
days as they transmit all they have learned that has been
passed on to them throughout the generations.[271]

Samuel Doe and Emmanuel Habuka Bombande, from the
West African Network for Education and Peace, explain that,
in the case of the Mali-Burkina Faso dispute, the

> *griot demonstrated what was fundamental to
> Africans when there is conflict: the relationship.
> Tracing the root of the relationship of the parties –
> and not the root of their conflict – takes precedence
> over all other processes. The griot was invited to look
> into time and evoke physically and spiritually the
> community to which the disputing nations belong.*[272]

---

[271] Banning Eyre/World Music Productions, *What Is a Griot?* (1997 [cited
August 15 2003]); available from http://artsedge.kennedy-
center.org/aoi/html/griot.html.

[272] Doe, "A View from West Africa," 167.

The *griot* is a specialist in the spoken/sung word and the power and energy it releases that animates the natural world.[273] Invoking the memory of their ancestors, the *griot* played a critical role in "the integration and reconciliation of time and events," reminding the presidents of *ile tempore*, or the beginning of time, when relations between the Supernatural and their communities were already established.[274] Through song and dance, the *griot* evoked regenerative forces, thereby allowing the presidents to let go of their mutual animosity and rather be guided by deeply held West African values and remain accountable to their ancestors.[275] Bringing the worldview of the two presidents forth, the *griot* reminded them of their shared norms and moral standards of justice, fairness, and their responsibilities to maintain community cohesion, cultural consistency, and public safety.

Reminding the presidents of their place and responsibility within the bigger picture, the *griot* encouraged the Malian and Burkinabé presidents to act in alignment with their "inherent human goodness." Inspiring personal integrity, the *griot* awakened in them a sense of their common humanity and "a means of tapping more fundamental sources of power."[276] As mentioned earlier Gandhi termed this internal power *satyagraha* which seeks not to defeat enemies, but rather to awaken them to their own humanity "by showing them the distress that their actions caused."[277] Drawing on the essence of what it means to be human, the warring presidents were able to relinquish the need to be right, end violent

---

[273] Banning Eyre/World Music Productions, *What Is a Griot?* ([cited August 15 2003]).

[274] Eliade, *Birth and Rebirth: The Religious Meanings of Initiation in Human Culture*, x.

[275] Doe, "A View from West Africa," 167.

[276] Peter Ackerman, *A Force More Powerful: A Century of Nonviolent Conflict*, 314.

[277] Ibid.

conflict, and "bring dignity instead of shame and suffering to their people."[278]

Clearly, assumptions about conflict and how it is handled may be appropriate in one culture but do not necessarily transfer to another.[279] In fact, exporting one conflict resolution model to another part of the world can have many dangerous repercussions. John Paul Lederach, came to the sobering realization that the underlying assumption in exporting Western conflict resolution models to other contexts is that the Western model is better and that Westerners have something to teach the rest of the world. Lederach realized that conflict resolution can sometimes include unintended imperialist attitudes and practices.[280]

For example, many Western approaches to conflict resolution may strengthen individualism rather than transform the heart of systems of domination or encourage interdependence between humans as well and all of creation. While there are a variety of mediation approaches used in the international community, the most dominant approach is interest-based negotiation, which is taught in the West and exported world-wide .[281] In this model, parties articulate the interests (needs, wants, fears, and values) underlying their positions.[282] Within this model, conflicting parties are encouraged to come up with creative solutions to address all parties' interests so that a "win-win" solution is achieved. In the West, this approach has been seen as a great improvement from a power-based approach, including the common law adversarial model that fosters "win-lose" solutions that tend to entrench

---

[278] Doe, "A View from West Africa," 164.

[279] John Paul Lederach, *Preparing for Peace: Conflict Transformation across Cultures* (Syracuse: Syracuse University Press, 1995), 38.

[280] After this realization Lederach developed the "elicitive" approach whereby practitioners draw on local conflict handling approaches. See Ibid.

[281] Roger Fisher, William Ury and Bruce Patton, *Getting to Yes: Negotiating Agreement without Giving In*, 2nd ed. (New York: Penguin Books, 1991).

[282] Ibid.

positions. While interest-based negotiation has been useful in some contexts, particularly in the Western hemisphere, it is important to understand its underlying assumptions, values, and ultimately its worldview.[283]

Bush and Folger explain that interest-based negotiation is rooted in an individualistic worldview where the ultimate value in personal and social life is individual satisfaction "because it means realizing life's potential for bringing fulfilment," and avoiding suffering.[284] To achieve these ends, rationality, direct communication, and efficiency are valued.[285] Essentially interest-based negotiation is utilitarian,[286] and its main goal is to resolve substantive issues. It does not however, address the context of systems of domination, injustice, greed, or the relational aspect of conflict.[287]

From a deeper cosmological perspective Western conflict resolution approaches are based on the Newtonian worldview of the universe as made up of separate objects acting in isolation. For example, each party is seen "as being an 'entity,' distinct from others, from nature, from God."[288] Moreover, interest-based negotiation is rooted in the social Darwinian belief that human nature is inherently self-interested and concerned with its own preservation and in competition over scarce resources. Finally, Descartes' separation of the mind

---

[283] Alan C. Tidwell, *Conflict Resolved? A Critical Assessment of Conflict Resolution* (London: Continuum, 1998).

[284] Bush, *The Promise of Mediation*, 236-42.

[285] Tidwell, *Conflict Resolved? A Critical Assessment of Conflict Resolution*, 26.

[286] Keashly, Loraleigh and Warters, William, "Working It Out: Conflict in Interpersonal Contexts," in *Patterns of Conflict Paths to Peace*, ed. Larry & Schellenberg Fisk (Peterborough: Broadview Press, 2000), 58; Catherine Morris, *Interests, Needs, Rights, Morality and Conflict Resolution* (2003 [cited November 2003]); available from http://www.peacemakers.ca/leadership/Morrisbib.html#papers.

[287] Morris, *Interests, Needs, Rights, Morality and Conflict Resolution* ([cited November 15 2003]).

[288] Vachon, "Beyond the Religion of Human Rights, the Nation State, and the Rule of Law," 8.

from emotions can be seen in interest-based negotiation as it focuses on the objective rational mind and considers emotions as something to be managed separately. Despite the dissonance with contemporary understandings of the universe as a continually unfolding and expanding living entity[289] and the human psyche's need for meaning and bonding,[290] the West not only clings to this approach but exports it worldwide.

Many non-Western dispute resolution practitioners, such as Mohammed Abu-Nimer,[291] George Irani,[292] and Sam Doe,[293] explain that these Western values and the underlying worldview counter their own cultural norms around conflict and community cohesion. They explain that community welfare is seen as paramount and individual responsibility lies not in gaining personal satisfaction, but rather in contributing their skills to ensure collective cohesion and harmony. Within their cultures, relationships, the expression of emotion, and the use of third parties such as elders, are valued over the substantive outcome. In these contexts, Western mediation such as interest-based mediation can inadvertently create cultural dissonance, erode local capacity, and ultimately fuel new sources of conflict.[294]

Remembering that reconciliation is essentially about transitioning from systems of domination to relationships of mutuality, conflict resolution practitioners must be mindful

---

[289] Thomas Berry in Farrell, "The Unfolding Story."

[290] Clark, *In Search of Human Nature*, 235.

[291] Mohammed Abu-Nimer, "Conflict Resolution Approaches: Western and Middle Eastern Lessons and Possibilities," *American Journal of Economics and Sociology* 55:35-52 55 (1996).

[292] George Irani, "Rituals of Reconciliation: Arab-Islamic Perspectives" (paper presented at the Centre for Religion and Society Lecture Series, University of Victoria, March 13 2002).

[293] Doe, "A View from West Africa," 168.

[294] Assefa, "Peace and Reconciliation as a Paradigm: A Philosophy of Peace and Its Implications on Conflict, Governance and Economic Growth," 30; Doe, "A View from West Africa," 168.

that their approaches are part of a larger global decolonization process that avoids imposing a Western worldview and works to strengthen cultural consistency, local capacity, and diversity. Choosing to use a *griot* to resolve the Mali-Burkina Faso border dispute can be seen as not only more effective but also contributes to rekindling and strengthening institutions that reflect uniquely African ways of knowing, doing, and being. As a result, eliciting local capacity strengthens cultural consistency, contributes to lasting cultures of peace, and regenerates global worldview pluralism.

Rather than exporting Western dispute resolution models that may inadvertently generate greater individualism, perhaps the West can learn from conflict handling approaches that inspire "transformation from the inside out" whereby people act in alignment with their highest ideals, their deepest cosmological beliefs, and in accordance with their "inherent human goodness." In this way, we can create global cultures of peace that foster meaningful existence, based on personal integrity, and an understanding that security is found in the quality of our relationships rather than in the quantity of our armaments.[295]

---

[295] Lederach, *The Journey Toward Reconciliation*, 202.

CHAPTER 3
WHEN WORLDS COLLIDE

*My initial reaction to arriving (in Mistissini):
"Now, what's up with these Cree? Are they mute
and do not speak? Are they taking the Mickey?
Such impolite activity!" In truth, the Cree didn't do
too much chattering, and a sort of tension was hov-
ering. Soon enough all was well and good. It was
this way for them, now we understood. It was not
us who taught them to speak, but rather they who
taught us to listen.*[296]

The Singing Mediator in the Mali-Burkina Faso example illustrates how engaging conflicting parties' fundamental worldviews can help create conditions for meaningful and lasting
reconciliation. But what happens when the fundamental
worldviews of the parties are not only different but actually
collide? How can dispute resolution and peace processes

---

[296] Maryse Demers, "Lend Me Your Shoes," *Cantilevers* 6 (1999): 53.

engage both worldviews and bridge conflict? This chapter starts with a brief first person narrative that illustrates the challenge of working through conflict when the parties' ways of framing reality, and hence code of ethics, differ. I then describe the following worldviewing skills: shifting worldview rigidity to flexibility; learning to listen for worldview difference; and creating shared pictures. Finally, I end with a story that illustrates how creating shared pictures between communities entrenched in deep-rooted conflict can lay the relational foundation for addressing difficult substantive issues and more meaningful reconciliation. These stories also illustrate that reconciliation is not an end goal but rather an on-going dynamic relationship "full of energy and differences."[297] In this way, rather than escalate conflict, worldview differences offer an opportunity to deepen one's own worldview and broaden one's understanding about life itself.

The Story of a Francophone-Cree Youth Exchange

In the 1990's I worked as a group leader for a youth intercultural exchange program called Chantiers Jeunesse. First Nations communities would invite this organization to bring six to twelve francophone youth from around the province of Quebec to their communities for the summer to participate in an intercultural exchange and to work on a community development project.[298] One of these exchanges was with Mistissini, a Cree community in northern Quebec. The youth band council initiated this project with the goal to improve francophone – Cree relations and strengthen Cree culture. Both groups were fighting for self-determination and often found themselves pitted against each another. Tensions were

---

[297] Assefa, "Peace and Reconciliation as a Paradigm: A Philosophy of Peace and Its Implications on Conflict, Governance and Economic Growth," 4.

[298] These youth exchanges were modelled after the European youth projects to reconstruct Europe after World War I and World War II. Their mission was to foster mutual understanding while reconstructing European infrastructures that had been demolished.

particularly high as the Oka crisis,[299] the fight over Hydro Quebec,[300] and the Quebec Referendum of 1995[301] played centre stage in recent years. The band council hoped an intercultural youth exchange project would help foster improved relations between the two groups and strengthen Cree culture.

As group leaders, my colleague and I brought six francophone youth to the community, who were then matched with six Cree youth. We lived together for the summer in the bush with an elder who taught us how to build a traditional Cree cultural camp. We learned how to prepare the land for a culture camp, build a large tipi and Chaptuan,[302] and most importantly how to live together in ways that valued worldview pluralism.

I learned that this project had been attempted the year before; however the Cree youth had left the project after only one week because of an underlying worldview conflict. With this in mind, I developed, along with my colleague, an extensive pre-departure orientation for the francophone youth, which included an intercultural skills module as well as presentations from resource people from Mistissini. When the Cree and francophone youth finally came together in Mistissini, my co-group leader and I carefully designed activities that reflected the differing culturally relevant ways of addressing group inclusion needs. For example, we balanced

---

[299] In 1990, there was an armed stand off between the Canadian army, the Securité Quebecois, and the Iroquois over land that the town of Oka wanted for a golf course and the Iroquois claimed was their traditional burial grounds.

[300] During the1990's the Cree fought against Hydro Quebec's plan to build a dam on their territories.

[301] In 1995, Quebec held a referendum to decide whether they would remain a part of Canada or separate. Many Indigenous people within the province of Quebec opposed separation as they were concerned about their own rights for self-determination.

[302] A Chaptuan is a large tent traditionally used for feasts and other important community gathering and events.

activities that were verbal and expressive to address francophone inclusion needs with more quiet and non-interference activities for the Cree youth.[303] What I learned from this
experience mostly relates to the francophone youth, I therefore make only occasional reference to the Cree experience.

Despite my best efforts, after about four days some of the
francophone youth came to me very upset and angry with
the Cree youth. Many wanted to leave. They complained
angrily that the Cree youth were not friendly, they never
looked them in the eyes or asked them questions. In addition,
some claimed, the Cree were lazy and never got up as early
to begin work. Finally, others were upset that in the day some
Cree youth would sleep on their beds. I realized that rudi-
mentary intercultural training was not enough. Worldviewing skills can only be developed in relationship.[304] No matter
how much we learn theoretically, when worldviews collide
our response is emotional.

The francophone youth demonstrated what is at the heart
of many relationships across worldview difference, particularly those with colonial histories. Rather than question oneself and one's own way of seeing and being in the world, the
youth's initial reaction was to dismiss, ridicule, and reject the
Cree youth's ways of seeing and being.

The francophone youth were exemplifying what Mary
Clark refers to as rigid worldviews; they could only see the
conflict from within their own framing of reality.[305] Clark has
examined worldviews throughout the world and has found
that some worldviews are more adaptable in the face of
change than others and can be seen on a continuum of

---

[303] Michelle LeBaron identifies three different ways to categorize cultural
starting points: high and low context communication; individualism and com-
munitarianism; and specificity and diffuseness. See LeBaron, *Bridging Cultural
Conflicts: A New Approach for a Changing World*.

[304] Marcos, *Our Word Is Our Weapon*, 391.

[305] Clark, *In Search of Human Nature*, 377.

rigidity to flexibility.[306] When a person (or community) who holds a **flexible** worldview encounters another person (or community) with a different worldview they are able to maintain their own worldview and learn about the other group's cosmology with ease and curiosity. On the other hand someone coming from a **rigid** worldview encountering another with a different cosmology will react by dismissing the difference as inferior or even wrong and proceed to impose their worldview through every means possible.[307] Going back to Nudler's thesis that worldviews hold the most fundamental and important human need for meaning, it is understandable that someone holding a rigid worldview would be very threatened by a different cosmology. Rather than questioning one's own worldview and hence the very meaning of one's existence, it is far easier to dismiss and try to dominate the other worldview.[308]

When "worlds collide," our code of ethics may be inadvertently violated, evoking deep feelings of indignation and even outrage.[309] In turn, strong emotions such as anger or outrage can activate the limbic system in our brain, which in turn transmits an adrenal message to either fight or flight.[310] For example, the francophone youth's indignation led them to feel victimized on the one hand, wanting to leave the project. On the other hand, they slipped into an offender role as they spoke in disrespectful ways about the Cree. In this way, a violation of deeply held principles can launch parties into a

---

[306] Ibid, Mary Clark, "Symptoms of Cultural Pathologies: A Hypothesis," in *Conflict Resolution Theory and Practice: Integration and Application*, ed. Dennis & van der Merwe Sandole, Hugo (Manchester and New York: Manchester University Press, 1993), 44-49; Clark, *In Search of Human Nature*, 379.

[307] This is particularly problematic when a person or group utilizes coercive means by drawing on economic, political, and military power sources unavailable to the other person or group.

[308] Redekop, *From Violence to Blessing: How an Understanding of Deep-Rooted Conflict Can Open Paths to Reconciliation*, 34.

[309] Clark, *In Search of Human Nature*, 188-89.

[310] Ibid., 217.

deep-rooted victim-offender cycle as each group's code of ethics is violated. In these circumstances, Redekop suggests that we must deal with the pain, break the trance,[311] and override our initial reactive responses in order to move relationships towards reconciliation.[312] Learning worldviewing skills that soften worldview rigidity and foster flexibility is a key element often overlooked but essential in transcending deep-rooted victim-offender cycles.

From Rigid to Flexible Worldviews

With a little guidance the francophone youth were able to quickly learn new worldviewing skills that enabled them to understand their own cultural lens, become aware of different ways of seeing and being in the world, and avoid spiralling into an endless victim-offender cycle. I listened to them fully and asked them to think about what offends them and try to identify what this told them about their own culture.

At first they resisted my suggestion because they were very angry and wanted to leave the program. I persisted and asked that one of their complaints was that the Cree never looked them in the eye and I wondered what that told them about their own culture. The participant that was most upset by this discovered that eye contact and a great deal of verbal communication were important to her. Without that she felt unwelcome and even rejected. Similarly, another participant began to discover that a certain amount of personal space is important to her and that she did not like other people lying on her bed. Finally, the participant who was the most upset about what he perceived as the laziness of the Cree youth discovered that he had a strong Protestant work ethic that

---

[311] See Redekop, *From Violence to Blessing: How an Understanding of Deep-Rooted Conflict Can Open Paths to Reconciliation*, 291.

[312] Ibid., 288-91.

placed a high value on being punctual and working long hours.[313] For many of the youth it was the first time they had identified specific values related to their culture.[314]

I then asked them to suspend judgment over the next few days and whenever they felt offended to think about what that said about their own values and culture and to also develop a sense of curiosity about what that may indicate is important to Cree culture. This was no easy task because the francophone youth genuinely felt excluded, rejected, and disrespected. Suspending judgment entails attending to and releasing emotional reactions and choosing instead an attitude of openness and curiosity.[315] In developing an openness to another worldview, the francophone youth were able to adjust their initial emotional responses and develop a sense of inquiry; they also gained knowledge about themselves and even life itself.

Learning To Listen To Worldview Difference

Soon, the francophone youth began to realize that the Cree youth have different notions of personal space, time, work ethics, and communication. For example, one youth told me she realized the lack of eye contact and verbal communication may indicate that the Cree value silence and could even demonstrate respect by allowing the francophone youth to fit into the larger group in the way they are most comfortable. By suspending judgment, she began to not only understand another worldview but also began to develop an appreciation for silence and non-interference. By the end of the project, both the francophone and Cree youth spent

---

[313] LeBaron explains that time and work is one of the most common intercultural misunderstanding; see LeBaron, *Bridging Cultural Conflicts: A New Approach for a Changing World*, 275.

[314] LeBaron explains nothing is culturally neutral and therefore it is important to understand your own cultural lens; see Ibid, 275.

[315] LeBaron describes these skills as developing a *spirit of inquiry* (awareness increases, perspective broadens, and starting points are explored) and a *spirit of release* (judgment does not block perception) in 2003, 142.

much of their time together enjoying shared silence. In fact, many francophone youth reported that after their return to their home communities, friends would ask why they were no longer talkative. In an interview with *The Cree Nation*, a francophone participant, Isabelle Gauthier, explained that after this project she no longer saw "the point in talking for the sake of talking."[316] This was certainly in stark contrast to the beginning of the project when many participants felt anxious with silence.[317] Robert Vachon explains that as we develop a rich and full inner life, we have less need to talk and instead discover "movement and growth in silence and stillness."[318]

Another youth realized that in his frenzy to work hard he missed opportunities to build quality relationships. He noticed that the Cree youth may not start work as early as him, but that they actually got a lot more done in a shorter amount of time because they talked together about the work and therefore came up with ways to accomplish tasks with less effort and more efficiency. Again Isabelle Gauthier explained that at first she thought the "Crees are unorganised compared to non-Natives. But (now) I feel it is the opposite, that non-Natives get too stressed out by deadlines. It is something that I learned, just relaxing around time."[319] In essence, the Cree taught the francophone youth the art of *being* rather than *doing*.

Yet another youth who had been outraged about Cree youth sleeping on her bed begun to understand that different cultures have different notions of ownership, sharing, and

---

[316] William Nicholls, "Working Together Respecting Differences," *Nation* 3, no. 22 (1996): 12.

[317] Ibid.

[318] Vachon, "Beyond the Religion of Human Rights, the Nation State, and the Rule of Law," 7.

[319] Nicholls, "Working Together Respecting Differences," 11.

personal space.[320] She realized her culture values individually owned property whereas perhaps the Cree saw objects as something to be shared. While she still struggled with her emotional reaction, she was able to suspend judgment and become curious about another way of being and perceiving.

One participant began to feel Cree culture was better than francophone culture and began to reject francophone culture and adopt Cree ways. In his eagerness to "go Native," the Cree youth began to distance themselves from him. He learned that taking on another's culture created inauthentic relationships. Slowly he learned the importance of valuing his own culture and how to engage respectfully with another. In *Towards Ethnorelativism: A Developmental Model of Intercultural Sensitivity*, Milton Bennett describes the phenomenon of denigrating one's own culture and believing another culture as superior as "reversal."[321] Bennett explains that while this may appear to be a more enlightened stance than denigrating the other culture, in fact it is "only changing the center of ethnocentrism."[322] Bennett explains that "reversal" can be a normal developmental stage in learning intercultural skills; however in order to progress to more authentic relationships of mutuality, a person stuck at this stage must first learn to value his/her own culture.[323]

The youth had learned vital worldviewing skills. Rather than using their judgments as an excuse to reject others or

---

[320] Western culture sees property as individually owned, while many indigenous cultures traditionally do not have a concept of property rights, but rather a code of ethics that emphasizes one's responsibility to use things "in a spirit of harmonization with all that exists" in Vachon, "Beyond the Religion of Human Rights, the Nation State, and the Rule of Law," 13.

[321] Milton Bennett, "Towards Ethnorelativism: A Developmental Model of Intercultural Sensitivity," in *Education for the Intercultural Experience*, ed. Michael Paige (Yarmouth: Intercultural Presss, 1993), 19; Vachon, "Beyond the Religion of Human Rights, the Nation State, and the Rule of Law."

[322] Bennett, "Towards Ethnorelativism: A Developmental Model of Intercultural Sensitivity," 20.

[323] Ibid., 21.

themselves, they learned to use these strong emotions, such as indignation, as a map to better understand their own culture and that of the Cree. Marcos explains, "by listening and learning about the differences of the other, (we can) understand better what (is) different in us."[324] Building relationships across differences provides an opportunity to strengthen, appreciate, revise, and at times re-make our worldviews.[325]

This was a turning point for the group; they began to build truly mutual relationships with one another. While during the previous year all Cree youth had left the project, this year dozens of Cree youth soon joined the project. In addition, as the francophone youth became more inquisitive about Cree ways and culture, the Cree youth developed a sense of curiosity and interest in their own culture, igniting a new thirst for knowledge and connection to their own roots.

Creating Shared Pictures

Soon the group began to develop shared pictures,[326] they were able to be loyal to their own worldviews, yet develop ways to work and live together that reflected a truly intercultural environment. For example, each youth led different aspects of the project and had to consider the various world frames within the group. One of the Cree youth took on coordinating work responsibilities for the entire group. Sometimes he encouraged the francophone youth to slow down, take time to enjoy what they were working on, and the people they were working with. Likewise, he would motivate some of the Cree youth to get up earlier to begin work with everyone.[327] At the beginning of the project, English was the common language; however as relationships developed

---

[324] Marcos, *Our Word Is Our Weapon*, 391.

[325] LeBaron discusses this practice as attunement and alignment. See LeBaron, *Bridging Cultural Conflicts: A New Approach for a Changing World*, 170.

[326] Shared pictures is a term used in Ibid., 291.

[327] Nicholls, "Working Together Respecting Differences," 11.

French, Cree, and English were used interchangeably and sometimes all within the same sentence.

Creating an environment where everyone's way of framing reality was valued led the francophone youth to develop a new awareness of and empathy for the experiences of the Cree youth. In the evenings, we frequently shared stories around a campfire or went to the nearest town for an evening of dancing. Campfire stories included traditional legends imbued with metaphor and proverbs as well as personal experiences and sometimes even song. [328] For example, near the end of the project, two Cree youth shared their experiences of being called "stupid lazy Indians" when they went to the neighbouring white school. Francophone youth began to see how rigid worldviews can easily degenerate into cruel racist comments like these and understood better the importance of learning worldviewing skills as a way to humanize relationships across difference.

Some evenings we canoed across the lake to the reserve. From the reserve we took a mini van down a dirt road for one and a half hours until we reached the neighbouring francophone town, Chibougamoo, where we went dancing. As frequently happened, when the bar closed a fight broke out between Cree and francophone youth from the region. Regardless of whether francophone or Cree youth had started the fight, the police would often arrest the Cree youth. While participants from our program were never arrested, this deeply affected the francophone youth as they witnessed

---

[328] Storytelling metaphors, legends, myths, proverbs, and song are all windows into a person or culture's worldview; see LeBaron, *Bridging Cultural Conflicts: A New Approach for a Changing World*, 275-83. For example, during environmental negotiations a developer may refer to a forest as a "farm" to be clearcut; whereas a conservationsist may refer to the same forest as apart of our "living planet" to be preserved. Each metaphor gives us a clear image the relationship each person has to the forest and conveys a glimpse into their meaning-making worlds in Docherty, *Learning Lessons from Waco: When the Parties Bring Their Gods to the Negotiation Table*, 290.

first hand injustices inflicted on people they had come to love.[329]

Worldviewing skills go beyond improving interpersonal relationships, they have the capacity to deepen our own cultural roots, broaden our understanding of life, and ultimately develop the fullness of our humanity. Moreover, creating shared pictures that first work to open the heart and build relationships can generate a kind of creative tension leading to innovative ideas – an important ingredient in transforming deep-rooted inter-community conflicts and laying conditions for meaningful and lasting reconciliation. To illustrate this potential, I will end this section with an inspiring story about how a community play transformed the relationship between Enderby, a small predominantly white rural town in the Okanagan, and the neighbouring Splats'in First Nation.

Not The Way I Heard It

Cathy Stubington, a Euro-Canadian puppet theatre artist, moved to Enderby, a small town in the north Okanagan in 1994. She was unsure what she could do with her skills and how she could contribute to this town. After having three children in two years, she eventually initiated, with the support of a steering committee, a project called *The Enderby and District Community Play Project*. The idea for the project was modelled after English playwright and director Anne Jellicoe's work in which "a core group of professional theatre artists work in a community for a period of time to facilitate

---

[329] An ethic of love in peace-building, community building, and dispute resolution is explored in the following texts: Elise; Brigagao Boulding, Clovis; Clements, Kevin., "Practice Love and Sustain Hope," in *A Handbook of International Peace-building: Into the Eye of the Storm*, ed. John Paul and Jenner Lederach, Janice (San Francisco: Jossey -Bass, 2002), 299-304; Clark, *In Search of Human Nature*, 221-28; bell hooks, *All About Love: New Visions* (New York: William Morrow and Company, Inc., 2000), 86-101.

and create a play about the community, for the community, and put it together with as many members of the community as possible."[330] The play's story line is drawn from local people's real lived experiences. As Stubington gathered stories, she realized there was something significant missing – the voices and stories from the neighbouring Splats'in First Nation. Moreover, she realized that since moving to this town, like many others in Enderby, she had never even talked to one person from this First Nation community. Like many rural communities in Canada, the lines between First Nations and Euro-Canadian cultures are solidly drawn. Racism runs deep and contact is often minimal.[331] She was unsure what to do about this but decided that the play would only be successful if it managed to bridge this gap.

Eventually, Stubington contacted the Splats'in band office to discuss her play and the possibility of their participation. Soon she was invited to a band council meeting, which eventually led her to build good relationships with the community. As she got to know the community, the more she realized how different their cultures were, and the less sure she became on how to proceed. Her persistence, however, paid off. She was finally introduced to the Splats'in story-keeper,[332] Rosalind Williams. Trust was built incrementally as they found ways to work together in a spirit of equality and respect for their respective perspectives. As Stubington became aware that it would be inappropriate to write the First Nations segments herself, she asked Williams if she

---

[330] Cathy Stubington, "A Panel Discussion on Cultural Development" (paper presented at the Creative Cities Network Inaugural Conference, Morris J.Wosk Centre for Dialogue, Vancouver, November 2003).

[331] Dorothy Christian, personal communication, December 2003.

[332] A story-keeper is responsible for keeping stories about the community, its members, and the land. Based on an oral tradition, the story-keeper must have an impeccable memory as she or he must remember who is related to whom, how the community relates to other communities, and to the land and to resources; Dorothy Christian, e-mail communication, January 15, 2004.

would like to co-write the play, along with herself and Vancouver director and playwright James Fagan Tait,[333] so that each depicted, to the best of their ability, the history of both communities from their respective worldviews and experiences. Their hope was to involve both community members as a way to build relationships and raise consciousness about their joint histories. They involved approximately eight hundred people from both communities, a spectrum from sectors such as education, health, police, government, small business, and the service industry. One hundred and sixty-three community members took acting roles; three hundred or more volunteered as seamstresses, set designers, and construction builders; and hundreds more donated items for the play, told stories or participated in workshops.[334] Working together they built relationships where previously there had been none.[335]

Finally, in 1999, they presented their play, entitled *Not The Way I Heard It*. The play was sold out virtually every night for two weeks as community members from both Enderby, Splats'in, and elsewhere filled the seats to attend the performance. One Splats'in community member, Dorothy Christian attended several rehearsals and two performances in order to make a video of the play entitled *One Small Step*. She recounts being particularly moved when she saw young men from her own community, who are normally busy partying and rarely engage in community events, actively participate as actors. For her, their participation showed their pride in seeing their own stories on stage. One night Christian sat next to an elderly white man from Enderby. She noticed during the part of the play that depicted the creation of the reserve and the impact European arrival had on First Nations, he cried. She was deeply touched to see that the history of her people had an impact on him. The response of this man and its effect on

---

[333] James Fagan Tait is playwright and director from Vancouver.

[334] Cathy Stubington, December 2003.

[335] Dorothy Christian, "One Small Step," (Vancouver: 1999/2000 season).

Christian illustrates that when we realize the depths of what has been lost, we can find our common humanity in shared pain.[336] In opening our hearts, we tap into our deeper selves where there is a wellspring of love that connects us to the rest of humanity.[337]

This play became a vehicle for creating a shared picture between these two previously antagonistic cultures. As a result, the two communities have continued to build relationships, slowly moving towards creating conditions for more substantial reconciliation. For example, in 2001, the Splats'in band held their 17th annual Secwepemc (Shuswap) nation annual gathering. For the first time, they invited the three neighbouring non-Native municipalities. Euro-Canadians were so surprised that many phoned the Splats'in band office to ensure they were truly invited. Christian recounts the gathering's first day where her community fed over six hundred people, including many Euro-Canadians. She was particularly surprised to see her grade one teacher who came to seek her out and participate in the festivities.

In 2002, Cathy Stubington was concerned that the British Columbia referendum on treaty negotiations[338] would undermine the hard community building work they had achieved. She went to the band office to discuss her concerns with Chief Gloria Morgan. Together they decided to hold a public meeting to clarify the issues for both communities. They held it at the band hall and invited various speakers. The idea was to bring both cultures together again to discuss common issues and voice concerns. To their surprise, over two thirds attended from outside of the band, a first in the history of the two communities.

---

[336] Parry, *Warriors of the Heart*, 12-13.

[337] Carl Jung, *Memories, Dreams, Reflections* (New York: Vintage Books, 1965), 396; Parry, *Warriors of the Heart*, 38.

[338] In 2002, the government of British Columbia held a referendum for all residents to vote on the breadth and scope of First Nations treaty negotiations. The process and wording was widely seen as a way to further undermine indigenous claims to land, resources, and self-government. See Alfred, *Deconstructing the British Columbia Treaty Process* ([cited December 10 2003]).

Similarly, within Enderby and other non-Native neighbouring towns there has been a push, albeit supported by
case law,[339] to include First Nations in resource management
discussions. While these changes have been incremental, and
not always perfect, the relational shift has been remarkable
given the short time frame and long history of animosity
between the communities.

Last summer, Chief Gloria Morgan of the Splats'in band
and Mayor Sue Philipps of Enderby led the 2003 Canada Day
parade, sitting side by side in a convertible. Christian comments that on one level this act was politically difficult, given
the history of Canadian encroachment on their land and the
continued lack of acknowledgement and redress. However,
she also recognizes that on a symbolic level it has tremendous
significance. For example, she explains, "a little kid watching
the parade would see the Chief and mayor leading a parade
together. In the child's mind it would symbolize equality."[340]

For Christian, reconciliation is about stepping out of the
"politically correct box." Rather than jump to the conclusion
that the Chief has been co-opted into a Canadian nationalist
narrative, Christian argues it is important to understand that
some activities are small steps towards righting our relationships, but do not reflect an end in and of themselves.[341] In
fact, political correctness can sometimes foster inauthentic
relationships and result in false reconciliation. For example,
the term "First Nations" gives an impression of Indigenous
nationhood, while in practice Indigenous people are treated
as an ethno-cultural minority group holding special rights
within the Canadian state.[342] Similarly, one can apologize
using politically correct language but do little in terms of
changing relationships of domination. Reconciliation is not
an intellectual process; "the head can set direction for the

---

[339] *Delgamuukw V. British Columbia,* [1997], 3S.C.R.1010.

[340] Christian.

[341] Ibid.

[342] Taiaiake Alfred, personal communication, November 15 2002.

heart, but the heart must arrive at its own pace."[343] Going through the motions of reconciliation with our words, when our heart firmly disagrees, can actually worsen relationships as resentment festers over time.[344] Chief Avrol Looking Horse, a Lakota elder explains, "the longest road you'll ever walk in your life is the sacred journey from your head to your heart."[345] Bypassing this journey can create internal dissonance and "simply halt us at that point" in the reconciliation process.[346] Reconciliation is a whole-hearted process that involves authenticity and self-responsibility. Only in engaging the mind, heart, body,[347] and spirit[348] can conditions be created for reconciliation.

These small steps toward reconciliation can sometimes lead to surprising results. For example, a few months before the opening night, the steering committee of the Enderby-Splats'in play decided to hold a *Floating Lantern Ceremony* in celebration of British Columbia River Day on the river that runs through the two communities. Cathy Stubington, with the help of two youth, held several lantern-making workshops prior to the event. In addition, the committee decided to ask someone from each community to speak about the river at the ceremony. A gift was given to two elders from the Splats'in community with this request. In the end the Splats'in drum group sang, Elder Lena Bell prayed in the Secwepemc language, and someone from the municipality of Enderby talked about the river. They then each launched

---

[343] Dunn, "The Process of Forgiveness-an Excercise," 31.

[344] Ibid.

[345] Chief Arvol Looking Horse, *A Call to Action* (2001 [cited December 15 2003]); available from
http://www.cleannorth.org/article/312.html?mode=nocomment.

[346] Dunn, "The Process of Forgiveness-an Excercise," 31.

[347] Redekop, *From Violence to Blessing: How an Understanding of Deep-Rooted Conflict Can Open Paths to Reconciliation*, 302.

[348] Dorothy Christian, personal communication, December 10, 2003.

their lanterns.[349] The event was so successful that it has become an annual event. For Dorothy Christian, learning about this event was a particularly hopeful sign because, for her, reconciling with the land is at the heart of Indigenous – non- Indigenous reconciliation.[350]

These two stories illustrate how the creation of shared pictures and reconciliation are not "one time events" or an end goal where one finally arrives. Rather reconciliation is an on-going dynamic relationship, "full of energy and differences."[351] The Cree-francophone youth exchange and the Enderby-Splats'in play illustrate being rooted in one's own worldview, developing the capacity to dynamically engage with another worldview, and creating shared pictures lays a relational foundation for taking risks, generating innovative ideas, addressing substantive issues, and building relationships of mutuality.

Like with building blocks, we draw on our previous worldviewing skills and continually learn more. For example, the dominant cultural group begins to realize that there are other ways of thinking, seeing, and framing reality and starts to learn the humility involved in being part of humanity rather than in charge of it. Similarly, the cultural group that has been on the receiving end of cultural domination begins to recognize institutions and conflict resolution initiatives that do not resonate with their meaning-making systems and seek to connect with their own. Both groups work at honing their worldviewing skills; they learn new freedom in staying loyal to their unique ways of seeing and knowing while simultaneously engaging and connecting with other world frames. Together

---

[349] Cathy Stubington, email communication, March 17, 2004

[350] Christian, personal communication, March 22, 2004. For more information on the importance of reconciling with the land see Dorothy Christian, "Witness," ed. Dorothy Christian (Vancouver: Vision Skylight, 1998).

[351] Assefa, "Peace and Reconciliation as a Paradigm: A Philosophy of Peace and Its Implications on Conflict, Governance and Economic Growth," 4.

they deepen their respective worldviews and learn how to foster shared pictures.

As both groups develop fuller pictures, everyone begins to realize the enormity of what has been lost.[352] When we fully face the current global cultural crisis, whereby eliciting local capacity after it has been eradicated, forgotten, or damaged beyond recognition seems next to impossible, we can easily become overwhelmed. Moreover, regenerating meaning and flexibility into Western worldviews (or other dominating cultures) seems like a monumental task given the current global monoculture and chaos. Rekindling worldview pluralism however, is an imperative as it is "akin to healing the spirit that sustains us."[353] Anchoring ourselves in the vision of a vibrant and pluralistic world and remembering cultural resiliency illustrated by Rigoberta Menchu's words when she says, "you have taken away the foliage and branches and even the trunk of our (cultural) tradition, but we still have our roots," [354] we can gather strength and courage to undertake this necessary journey. It is to this task that I shall now turn.

---

[352] Joseph Montville writes about the importance of healing the wounds of history through storytelling and joint 'walks through history' in Montville, "Justice and the Burden of History," 129-43.

[353] Marie Battiste, ed., *Reclaiming Indigenous Voice and Vision* (Vancouver: UBC Press, 2000), xxiv.

[354] Esteva, "Enough, Basta" 84.in Vachon, "Guswenta or the Intercultural Imperative: Towards a Re-Enacted Peace Accord between the Mohawk Nation and the North American Nation-States (and Their People)," 54.

CHAPTER 4

OUT OF THE ASHES, PHOENIX RISES

Why should it always be up to the Native people to come to city courts of justice to defend their rights and never up to the "civilized" to prove their titles in Native courts? Western man might then find it a little difficult to prove his rights in duty-community-cosmic-oral tradition-wampum-oriented-courts as native people do in our courts based on civil law and written traditions.[355]

In the mid 1800's, a group of Hopi elders conducted a ceremony and were told that as Indigenous people they were in their midnight; however, they would eventually come into their daylight, and emerge as world leaders after the Eagle lands on the moon.[356] Despite this message seeming far-fetched at the time – who could imagine an eagle landing on

---

[355] Vachon, "Beyond the Religion of Human Rights, the Nation State, and the Rule of Law," 27.

[356] Hodgson, "Residential School: 'A Shared Journey' in Redefining Relationships," 2.

the moon – each generation passed down this prophesy.[357] Midnight for Indigenous people stretched over one hundred years in Canada and included outlawing cultural and spiritual practices, implementing assimilation policies such as residential school legislation, land encroachment, dismantling Indigenous governance structures, and widespread epidemics such as small pox.[358] Then in 1969 when the Americans landed on the moon the message they sent back to Earth was "the Eagle has landed." Soon afterwards the first alcohol and drug treatment centre was established, beginning a new era of healing and sobriety for Indigenous people.[359] During the same year, the Canadian government introduced the White Paper that attempted to usurp treaty responsibilities and take away special rights for Indigenous people. In response, First Nations across the country rose to the occasion, strongly opposing any attempt to assimilate Indigenous people into Canadian society. This was a significant landmark in fighting back and linking First Nations struggles with Indigenous movements worldwide.[360]

A second prophecy arose from a vision in 1990 during a sacred ceremony at an international Indigenous gathering in Quito Ecuador led by elders there.[361] They received a mes-

---

[357] Ibid

[358] Hodgson, "Residential School: 'A Shared Journey' in Redefining Relationships," 3&6. Sutherland, *Colonialism, Crime, and Dispute Resolution: A Critical Analysis of Canada's Aboriginal Justice Strategy* ([cited December 10 2003]).

[359] Hodgson, "Residential School: 'A Shared Journey' in Redefining Relationships," 10.

[360] Cole Harris, *Making Native Space: Colonialism, Resistance, and Reserves in British Columbia* (Vancouver and Toronto: University of British Columbia Press, 2002), 300; Leroy Little Bear et al., "Federal Policy and Indian Self-Government in Canada," in *Pathways to Self-Determination: Canadian Indians and the Canadian State*, ed. Leroy Little Bear et al., (Toronto, Buffalo, and London: University of Toronto Press, 1992), 70.

[361] Dorothy Christian, "Living the Prophesy," in *Insight*, ed. Dorothy Christian (Vancouver: Vision TV, 2001/2002), Hodgson, "Residential School: 'A Shared Journey' in Redefining Relationships," 13.

sage from the fire that healing and reconciliation would come when the Eagle and the Condor came together around the time of the new millennium.[362] For them this symbolized the Indigenous people of the North, who view the Eagle as sacred, coming together with the Indigenous people of the south, who view the Condor as sacred.[363] In 1992, elders put the prophesy into action by having the first *Peace and Dignity Journey*. Indigenous runners ran south with Eagle staffs from the tip of Alaska, while other Indigenous runners ran north from the base of South America with Condor staffs to Mexico City where the two groups met and together went to Teotihauacan, the sacred location of the Temple of the Moon and Temple of the Sun. There, they performed sacred ceremonies to reclaim their right to pray and have ceremonies.[364] For many Indigenous people, Teotihauacan is considered the belly button of Mother Earth where knowledge and understanding for all of humanity is held. Reclaiming the right to pray and have ceremonies is key for the empowerment of Indigenous people and the healing of all of humanity.[365]

Since then, every four years *Peace and Dignity* runners travel the length of the Americas, each from opposing ends, meeting in Mexico City and proceeding together to Teotihauacan. In 2000, Dorothy Christian, a Shecewepemc (Shuswap) – Okanagan woman and documentary filmmaker, met them on their journey while they were in British Columbia, flew with a crew to Mexico City to film the ceremony where the runners from the north and the south joined together. United, they ran to Teotihauacn to the Temples of the Sun and the Moon, with Christian filming as they went.[366]

---

[362] Hodgson, "Residential School: 'A Shared Journey' in Redefining Relationships," 3.

[363] Christian, "Living the Prophesy."

[364] Ibid.

[365] Ibid.

[366] Ibid.

The *Peace and Dignity Journey* organizers endeavoured to walk their talk. They did not accept sponsorship from any tobacco, liquor, or oil companies as they felt these companies harmed humans and the environment. Moreover, the runners were asked to abstain from alcohol, drugs, and sex. When they ran with their Eagle staffs, with every step they prayed to the Earth or to the Sun. They believe that there is writing on the Earth that is unseen but felt. In praying as they ran they lay new writing on the Earth. An elder explains that the staff grew from Mother Earth and each Eagle feather represents direct connection to the Great Spirit. In addition, each Eagle staff represents a family or Indigenous community so the runners pray for this family or community as they run. The *Peace and Dignity Journey* endeavoured to link up to as many Indigenous communities along the way to spread the message of the prophecy as well as to learn about each other's cultures.[367]

The staffs lifted the runners' spirit when their bodies were tired or filled with internal conflict such as learning news of a death in their home communities. One of the runners, Zeta explains that running and breathing is akin to listening to the voice of your spirit. For him living in peace and dignity "starts with your own fire in your own home – with your own spouse, family, and all others including all of mankind, the Earth, and the elements of life. You take care of your own fire first so that you can step out in a dignified way for all these."[368]

In *The First Steps To Freedom*, Taiaiake Alfred suggests that meaningful Indigenous existence cannot be achieved solely from achieving self-determination and resurrecting traditional institutions. He illustrates that Indigenous disconnection from their lands and cultures have led to a spiritual crisis.[369] It follows, Alfred insists, that only a spiritual revolu-

---

[367] Ibid.

[368] Ibid.

[369] Taiaiake Alfred, *The First Steps to Freedom* (2002 [cited July 11 2002]); avail-

tion that addresses the consciousness of each individual will solve the problem. He calls on Indigenous people to "start acting on who our ancestors were, what they were like, and the things they believed."[370] For Alfred, being Indigenous is more than a label, "it means looking at the personal and political choices we make every day and applying an Indigenous logic to them. It means living in accordance with Kanien'kehaka, Innu, and Wet'suwet'en values; thinking and behaving in a way that is consistent with the laws of nature and the teachings of our ancestors."[371]

Like Indigenous people, Westerners are also experiencing profound dissonance between our worldview and our institutions and actions. Thomas Berry argues that the downfall of Western civilization has been our disconnection from the land. He explains that alienation towards nature happened following the Great Plague in the fourteenth century when over one third of Europe died. Without any scientific knowledge about germs and their transmission, people began to see nature as something to be controlled and to fear.[372]

Most historical Judeo-Christian interpretations of scripture reinforced this notion, believing humans to have dominion over the rest of creation. Galileo and Descartes laid the foundation for a rational worldview based on the belief in an objective reality that can be measured.[373] Newton inadvertently deepened our separation from nature claiming "all the entities in the universe are isolated, discrete objects that have distinct boundaries."[374]

Recent scientific insights have made it clear that humans are part of nature, yet our institutions and ways of being have yet

---

able from www.taiaiake.com/home/index.html.

[370] Ibid.

[371] Ibid..

[372] Thomas Berry in Baylands Production, "The Unfolding Story, " (1993).

[373] Abram, *The Spell of the Sensuous*, 3.

[374] Clark, *In Search of Human Nature*, 11.

to catch up with this new awareness.[375] We now know, thanks to Einstein and later Hubble,[376] that the universe is not static but rather is constantly expanding with its own internal dynamic. Moreover, the recent discovery that the atom has a vast inner dimension and presence that acts on its own accord has shifted our awareness from believing only humans have free will to the possibility that all of creation has its own internal dynamism. Finally, landing on the moon gave us a new vantage point of the Earth as a living being that we are a part of rather than something we can control. We now know that human beings are members of a larger universe and harming the Earth is ultimately harming ourselves. For example, experimenting with nuclear capacities on the Marshall Islands has resulted in subsequent generations of birth defects, cancer, and high mortality rates. Similarly, nuclear accidents such as Chernobyl have had long term effects beyond the borders of the former Soviet Union and has contaminated Canada's north. Moreover, biologist Mary Clark argues that history shows that human survival is not primarily based on competition and self-interest as some social Darwinists suggest, but on cooperation, interdependence, and generosity.[377]

Essentially, Western culture has come full circle. Science has in fact helped us develop a greater certainty about our interconnectedness with nature, the mystery of an expanding and emerging universe, and the internal dynamism found in all of creation. Despite these insights, we as Westerners have yet to adapt our institutions or way of life in a way that reflects our new cosmology. Mary Clark explains that a culture that fails to change its perception of "how to live" eventually self-destructs.[378] Effective change, therefore, must first

---

[375] Fritjoff Capra, *The Turning Point* (New York: Simon and Schuster, 1982); Thomas Berry in Baylands Production, "The Unfolding Story, " (1993).

[376] Einstein proved the universe is not static and Hubble confirmed his hypothesis with his invention of a powerful telescope.

[377] Clark, *In Search of Human Nature*, 102, 22, 23.

[378] Ibid., 285.

start with the consciousness of individuals for a cohesive Western culture to regenerate and re-civilize itself.

Within every culture there are rituals, legends, prophesies, creation stories, and myths that offer insights into the cyclical nature and rise and fall of eras and cultures. They provide roadmaps on how to surf the waves of turbulent times of transition and change.[379] Like the Indigenous prophesies, the legend of the Phoenix also conveys the understanding and experience that one must first journey inward and symbolically "die unto oneself" to enable a new and stronger culture and people to emerge. The legend of the Phoenix originated in Greece; however there are various versions around the word. The Phoenix is a solitary and unique bird that cannot reproduce. After approximately five hundred years, the Phoenix prepares for its own death and builds a nest to set itself on fire. Once the Phoenix has died and three days have passed, the new stronger offspring rises out of the ashes, embalms its predecessor, and transports it to the sun.[380] While cultural genocide is certainly a far cry from a natural process of the rise and fall of various cultures, we can nonetheless glean some insights from the Phoenix, the Eagle and the Condor, and other similar stories that emphasize the use of rituals for transformation.

Deep-rooted conflict erodes the way people make meaning out of life. It shakes beliefs about order, justice, fairness, and acceptable behaviour.[381] In the aftermath of cultural genocide, spiritual practices are sometimes lost, making healing from the resulting traumas difficult. In addition, deep-rooted conflict fosters pervasive suspicion, fear, and distrust amongst

---

[379] Joseph Campbell, *Creative Mythology: The Masks of God* (New York: Penguin Books, 1968), 282-92; Eliade, *Birth and Rebirth: The Religious Meanings of Initiation in Human Culture*, 103-36; Christina and Stanislav Grof, *The Stormy Search for Self* (New York: Jeremy P. Tarcher/Putnam, 1990), 115-41.

[380] See Appendix IV for a version of this legend.

[381] Herman, *Trauma and Recovery: The Aftermath of Violence-from Domestic Abuse to Political Terror*, 35; Redekop, *From Violence to Blessing: How an Understanding of Deep-Rooted Conflict Can Open Paths to Reconciliation*, 36.

people, destroying the very fabric of society itself.[382] In damaging community cohesion and rupturing members' sense of connectedness and belonging, people begin to "seek security by identifying with something close to their experience and over which they have some control," such as identity groups linked to ethnicity or religion.[383] Social change agents themselves are not immune to widespread breakdown in relationships.[384] Infighting, hoarding of information, competition over resources, territoriality, and harsh judgements about each other's strategies or personal motives are all too pervasive. Creating conditions for lasting reconciliation requires attentiveness to the human psychic need for meaning, connectedness, and belonging.[385]

Michelle LeBaron explains that rituals fulfil our need for meaning and connectedness and "provide an anchor for what we have experienced deeply and what we wish to live into being."[386] In addition, rituals make "us feel secure in times of change or transition"[387] and help us connect the past, present and future. They draw on regenerative forces,[388] assisting people to shift identities from enemy to friend or from victim to creator.[389] Moreover, they draw on feelings and sensations,[390] providing an important vehicle for mourning losses and creating conditions for individuals

---

[382] Herman, *Trauma and Recovery: The Aftermath of Violence-from Domestic Abuse to Political Terror*, 214; Lederach, *Building Peace: Sustainable Reconciliation in Divided Societies*, 18.

[383] Lederach, *Building Peace: Sustainable Reconciliation in Divided Societies*, 13.

[384] Lederach, "Frontier Luncheon".

[385] Clark, *In Search of Human Nature*, 233.

[386] Michelle LeBaron, *Bridging Troubled Waters: Conflict Resolution from the Heart* (San Francisco: Jossey-Bass, 2002), 256.

[387] Ibid., 255.

[388] Eliade, *Birth and Rebirth: The Religious Meanings of Initiation in Human Culture*, 19.

[389] LeBaron, *Bridging Cultural Conflicts: A New Approach for a Changing World*, 279.

[390] Ibid., 211.

and their collectivities to rise Phoenix-like out of the ashes.

Eisenbruch coined the term "cultural bereavement" to explain the need for cultures to grieve the loss of their social structures, cultural values, and self-identity.[391] Psychological research on refugee groups demonstrate that "the failure to enact cultural rituals during and after a collective traumatic event" can lead to prolonged Post Traumatic Stress Disorder (PTSD) making it difficult to continue daily living.[392] For example, research with Cambodian refugees shows that those that fled to the United States, where the pressure to conform to the American "melting pot" is high, have more persistent PTSD symptoms that those who went to Australia where there is more tolerance for cultural diversity and the performance of cultural rituals.[393]

Vamik Volkan describes "chosen traumas" as a way to explain how trauma is passed down the generations solidifying victim identities, until they are fully grieved. Rupert Ross explains, "abuse gets passed from generation to generation, multiplying as it goes, until entire communities become engulfed by it."[394] Regenerative rituals offer opportunities to grieve losses and are best when accompanied by a "re-storying" of narratives. In creating joint narratives that reflect the fullness of shared stories, the never-ending victim-offender cycle can eventually be transcended.[395]

Within every culture there are collective mourning rituals. Drawing on these rituals helps communities mourn their losses and begin to prepare for the new, stronger and more resilient forms cultures will take. In *Peace, Power, and*

---

[391] M Eisenbruch, "From Post-Traumatic Stress Disorder to Cultural Bereavement: Diagnosis of Southeast Asian Refugees," *Social Science and Medicine* 33 (1991): 674.

[392] Mary de Young, *Collective Trauma: Insights from a Research Errand* (1998 [cited October 2003]); available from http://www.aaets.org/arts/art55.htm.

[393] Ibid.

[394] Ross, *Returning to the Teachings: Exploring Aboriginal Justice*, 39.

[395] Clark, *In Search of Human Nature*, 38-39.

Righteousness: an Indigenous manifesto, Alfred describes the Rotinohshonni ritual of condolence as a way for Indigenous people to rekindle worldview pluralism, transform loss into strength, foster a culture of peace, and re-establish autonomy for Indigenous people.[396] Alfred explains that the beginning of the ritual involves celebrating Indigenous resiliency followed by "a lament for the loss of knowledge and acknowledgement of what Indigenous people had in the past. In this way the ground is prepared by invoking the healing spirit of the condolence. It is necessary to clear cloudy emotions to make a strong and honest appraisal of the situation."[397] Invoking the healing spirit, Alfred explains, recognizes the enormity of the task at hand and gives direction for the mind and heart. Next, "requickening" describes how to bring traditional Indigenous teachings back to life and regenerate the authentic spirit of Indigenous people. Finally, Alfred advocates for "righteousness" that avoids the dangers of cooptation through developing personal integrity and loyalty to Indigenous worldviews and values.[398]

Indigenous regeneration is directly linked to a Western re-civilizing process. As Euro-Canadians learn about First Nations experiences they are often reminded of their own history and tap into their own unmourned losses. For example, at a gathering entitled *Pilgrimage Towards Right Relationships*, an Irish-Canadian participant linked First Nations experiences of land encroachment and poverty to his own history of British colonialism and the potato famine. He was surprised to feel, for the first time, grief over his own historic cultural losses and began to connect in a deeper way to First Nations experiences. Similarly, a small Anglican group met Tuesday evenings for five weeks in Victoria comparing early Celtic spirituality to First Nations' as well as to their similar experi-

---

[396] Alfred, *Peace, Power, and Righteousness: an indigenous manifesto*, xx-xxii.

[397] Ibid., xxiii.

[398] Ibid.

ences with colonialism. Going back to their own roots, participants discovered elements of Celtic spirituality that can help Western civilization's current cultural crisis.

Herbert O'Driscoll argues that Celts' nearness to nature, their use of nature for healing, their connectedness to God, their abundance of sacred places, their rich storytelling tradition, their understanding that life is a constantly changing journey, and a willingness to venture into the unknown can be useful today as we move out of the era of Enlightenment.[399] As Westerners retrieve the memory of their earliest ancestors, they begin to grieve their lost connection to the Earth as well as become invigorated to lead more meaningful and authentic lives.

As both Indigenous and Western peoples tap into their own wellspring of losses, they also come together to grieve. For example, in Australia a public memorial to commemorate the *Stolen Generation*[400] was developed by Aboriginal and non-Aboriginal people as a symbol of their collective grief and commitment to building a different future. The opening took place in May 2004 and was accompanied by extensive commemorative events. Through a series of public consultations the wording and design were decided in a spirit of consensus. It's heading reads, *They Took Our Children Away*, a recorded song with the same title greets visitors, quotes by survivors are displayed, a plaque reads, "this place honours all who have suffered under these policies. It also honours all those Indigenous and non-Indigenous, whose genuine care softened the tragic impact of what are now recognised as cruel and misguided policies."[401] Finally,

---

[399] Herbert O'Driscoll, "The Raven and the Dove" (paper presented at the The Greater Victoria Lay School of Theology, Christ Church Cathedral, November 25 2003).

[400] *The Stolen Generation* refers to Aboriginal children who were forcibly removed to attend residential school in Australia.

[401] John Bond, "A Strategy for a Real Australia," *Australian Newsbriefs*, October 2003.

there is a bench nearby that offers opportunities for contemplation.

Knowing when to remain still is an essential skill in the art of reconciliation and regenerating worldview pluralism after cultural genocide or any traumatic event. In order to learn stillness, one must first learn to resist clinging to the past and to resist the temptation to fix the present or grasp towards the future. Robert Shreiter cautions us to resist holding on to what has been lost. He explains,

> *Our first impulse may be to envision the move from violence and suffering as a step back to the way things might have been prior to the cataclysmic events that have wracked our societies and our lives. And some people have tried to do that. But a little experience and a little reflection teach us rather quickly that it is not possible. It is not only that the flow of time makes retrieving the past ultimately impossible; it is also that the experience of violence and suffering has changed us irrevocably. We are not the same people we were, so any return is not a return; it is coming into a new place. Those who have found themselves in the midst of war and violence cannot return to a prior, tranquil state. The violence of those times are burned into memory —repressed perhaps, but surely able to come to surface once again to haunt and horrify the present.*[402]

In addition to the dangers of prolonged PTSD previously mentioned, un-grieved losses can also lead to rigid fundamentalism or a fanaticism to resurrect the past. Rather than confront the unknown or stay with the discomfort of the void, parties grasp on to the old, even when it has become irrelevant to current circumstances and outmoded given the changing times. Essentially, this releases them "behaviourally

---

[402] Schreiter, *Reconciliation: Mission & Ministry in a Changing Social Order*, 11.

and ideologically from an intolerable complexity that cannot be managed or used in a more productive way."[403] In this way, they fill their inner void with meaning and identity. Psychological studies of "terrorist"[404] leaders show that many use violence as a means to achieve their human psychic needs for belonging, autonomy, and meaning.[405] A rigid ethnic identity helps create an internal cohesion, where once there was dissonance and alienation, giving a sense of meaning and purpose.[406] Vamik Volkan interviewed several "terrorist" leaders and discovered each had early trauma and boundary violation from beatings, sexual abuse, or abandonment. Clearly there are also political and economic reasons that motivate their behaviour. However, rigid identity, Volkan explains, gives them a longed-for sense of belonging. In addition, they are often admired and supported by various organizations and even countries, fulfilling their yearning for recognition and autonomy.[407] In fact, many such leaders will sabotage peace processes even when the accords address their professed goals. Volkan suggests that if an accord is to be successful, these leaders need alternative avenues to fulfil their need for belonging, recognition, and meaning. Clearly, successful peace processes must include ways to address these fundamental human needs.[408]

Recognizing and ritualizing the transition from one era to

---

[403] M. deVries, "Trauma in Cultural Perspective," in *Traumatic Stress*, ed. A.C. McFarlane B.A. van der Kolk, & L. Weisaeth (New York: The Guilford Press, 1996), 407.

[404] The term "terrorist" is very controversial. One person's terrorist is another person's freedom fighter. Moreover, the term terrorism tends to focus on individual acts of terror at the exclusion of state terrorism. I prefer to use the word "political violence" as it is more specific and includes the variety of forms it takes.

[405] Volkan, *Blood Lines: From Ethnic Pride to Ethnic Terrorism*, 161-64.

[406] Ibid., 160-61.

[407] Ibid., 162.

[408] Clark, *In Search of Human Nature*, 233; Volkan, *Blood Lines: From Ethnic Pride to Ethnic Terrorism*, 163.

another enables people to let go of the past and allow for the resurrection of stronger cultures to emerge with greater ease. Accepting that one cannot return to the past accompanies a similar journey in realizing that we can neither rescue nor be rescued. Imposing solutions from the outside, as mentioned earlier, may inadvertently further impose culturally biased solutions and erode the very worldviews we hope to rekindle. Moreover, deep-rooted conflict is sustained by a variety of roles people take such as victim, offender, bystander, accomplice, and hero/rescuer. Lasting reconciliation requires transcending these roles.[409] Intervenors must be mindful not to entrench the victim-offender-bystander-accomplice-rescuer roles[410] as the people themselves must nurture a new sense of internal power, self-responsibility, and openness that can eventually foster mutual understanding and even compassion.

Learning to live with ambiguity and relax into the unknown are essential skills in the regeneration of culture and creating conditions for reconciliation.[411] The ending of one era but before the birth of a new era calls on us to let go of the former ways of being and embark into the "not knowing", the void, or the Great Mystery. While we are often impatient with ambiguity and deeply uncomfortable with not knowing, "dwelling in that ambiguity may be necessary to keep us from repeating the past."[412] In fact, it is in the void that innovation, creativity and shared wisdom are born, enabling us to "transcend what exists, live with it, while creating something different."[413]

Every culture has ways to assist with a journey inward to the centre of our being where we are ultimately connected to

---

[409] see transcending victim-offender cycle in introductory chapter of this book for more details.

[410] LeBaron, *Bridging Troubled Waters: Conflict Resolution from the Heart*, 268-69.

[411] Ibid., 256.

[412] Schreiter, *Reconciliation: Mission & Ministry in a Changing Social Order*, 10.

[413] LeBaron, *Bridging Troubled Waters: Conflict Resolution from the Heart*, 255-56.

all of creation. For example, Indigenous practices such as the sweatlodge; Hindu traditions like yoga; and Zen Buddhist meditative states all help people journey inward. Similarly, Christian spiritual guidebooks such as *The Interior Castle*[414] and Sufi spiritual cartographies such as al-Harawi's *The Stages of Pilgrims Toward God* describe the soul's journey to maturity.[415]

Jung uses the term "individuation" to describe this transformative journey inward. He argues it is an essential part of becoming a fully mature human being. In letting go of our *persona*, healing our *shadow* through the willingness to feel our pain, and delving into the core of our being we discover a new depth to our authenticity and uniqueness. This journey does not shut others out, but rather "gathers the world to oneself."[416]

Mircea Eliade demonstrates how within cultures, rituals have been developed to not only journey to the centre of the self, but also symbolically re-enact a culture's creation stories, evoking a kind of "mystical death...(and an) occassion for total regeneration of the cosmos and the collectivity."[417] For example, *The Singing Mediator*, Christian baptism and communion rituals, puberty rites, and the Sun Dance are just a few examples of such regenerative rituals; indeed nearly every tradition has them.[418] What is common in most traditions is "the belief that a state cannot be changed without first being annihilated."[419] A temporary return to chaos and the repetition of the cosmogony[420] helps initiates let go of the old, journey to the centre of their being, and ultimately be created

---

[414] Grof, *The Stormy Search for Self*, 139.

[415] Ibid., 140.

[416] Ibid., 396.

[417] Eliade, *Birth and Rebirth: The Religious Meanings of Initiation in Human Culture*, 19.

[418] Ibid., 103-36.

[419] Ibid., xxiii.

[420] cosmogony refers to a culture's creation story.

anew.[421] Alfred explains that for Indigenous people, a powerful human being is someone who understands how to "gain access to natural power source through ritual...(and) at the height of power, there is a profound experience of oneness with nature."[422]

Sometimes, knowledge about rituals and collective healing has been lost. For example, many Indigenous spiritual practices, ceremonies, and rituals were outlawed in Canada. In this way, many Indigenous people had no means to heal from the traumas resulting from colonial policies.[423] As a result, intergenerational trauma and internal community factionalism ensued. Faced with this dilemma a Kwa'kwala'wakw woman suggests learning the basic principles embedded in the worldview/culture that has been lost "and then blend the contemporary and traditional together." [424] Recently a First Nations community in Alberta has done just that when they held a community validation process, which included a *Welcoming Home Ceremony*, for community members who had attended residential schools.[425] Maggie Hodgson explains,

> *That community has held a community validation process, which included groups of people who shared their stories about leaving home to go to residential school and about the emotional, spiritual, physical and sexual abuse, they suffered. Many people who attended this community validation have changed. One project worker has observed many participants' faces changing entirely after the community validation. There were many people who*

---

[421] Eliade, *Birth and Rebirth: The Religious Meanings of Initiation in Human Culture*, xxiii.

[422] Alfred, *Peace, Power, and Righteousness: an indigenous manifesto*, 50-51.

[423] Hodgson, "Residential School: 'A Shared Journey' in Redefining Relationships," 5.

[424] Alfred, *Peace, Power, and Righteousness: an indigenous manifesto*, 10.

[425] Hodgson, "Residential School: 'A Shared Journey' in Redefining Relationships," 39.

said, "Even if there is no legal resolution through ADR⁴²⁶ that community validation process was worth the struggle they had experienced with the development of the project. They wrapped up the community validation with a welcome home ceremony for all the students who attended residential school. The welcome home ceremony included a feast, prayers, traditional songs, sweat lodge ceremonies and a release of balloons with their residential school number on the balloons. The Chief watched his number float up into the sky until it disappeared and he said, "If I never get a penny this will have been worth it."⁴²⁷

Like many survivors of traumatic events, the vast majority of former residential school students have never been fully accepted by their community.⁴²⁸ For example, in an interview, Art Thompson, a well-known Nuu-chah-nuulth artist, explains that he had never been fully accepted in his home community despite his success with his art and his commitment to re-learn his culture and break free from his own personal victim-offender cycle he had been caught in for years.⁴²⁹ Community validation processes and welcoming home ceremonies, such as this one, are crucial for the healing of victims and the cohesion of devastated and divided communities. This example shows the creativity of a community to draw on

---

⁴²⁶ The current Alternative Dispute Resolution framework developed to address residential school grievances.

⁴²⁷ Hodgson 2003, 39.

⁴²⁸ For example when Holocaust concentration camp survivors first arrived in Israel after World War II they were placed in psychiatric wards – Haim Dasberg, *Myths and Taboos among Israeli First- and Second-Generation Psychiatrists in Regard to the Holocaust* (2000 [cited December 14 2003]); available from http://www.holocaustechoes.com/dasberg2.html; Volkan, *Blood Lines: From Ethnic Pride to Ethnic Terrorism.*

⁴²⁹ Taiaiake Alfred, *My Grandmother, She Raised Me up Again* (2003 [cited April 12 2003]); available from http://www.taiaiake.com/home/index.html.

healing traditions that remain, such as the sweat, feast, and prayers, as well as create new rituals and processes to address the lingering trauma on former students, their children, and other community members, such as in the sharing of residential school stories and releasing of balloons with residential school survivors' former student numbers.

In healing community rifts through the use of ceremony and storytelling, individuals, once rejected, recover the essential need to belong and create new meaning out of their common experiences. In turn, survivors regain their autonomy by developing their unique gifts and contribute them to the whole. This kind of intra-group reconciliation involves revising narratives in a way that reflects the diversity of experience within a community as well as helps victims come to terms with the past.[430] This is no easy task, as the victim-offender cycle not only exists between both victim and perpetrating groups, but also amongst victims themselves. For example, some students of residential schools perpetrated the abuse inflicted on them onto younger students. Other students were so damaged when they left residential school that they abused community members on their return. Some students, albeit not the norm, have good memories of residential school.[431] Creating shared pictures means developing inclusive narratives within a victim group as well as opportunities to celebrate resiliency and grieve losses.

In recent centuries, Western cultures have for the most part lost rituals as a regenerative source. Rituals today tend to mark endings and beginnings such as marriages, graduations, or funerals.[432] Even most churches perform rituals symbolically rather than regeneratively. Moreover, most dispute

---

[430] Stovel, "Unpublished Paper Reconciliation and Restorative Justice after Mass Atrocity: Clarifying Key Concepts", 20.

[431] Hodgson, "Residential School: 'A Shared Journey' in Redefining Relationships," 16; Ross, *Returning to the Teachings: Exploring Aboriginal Justice*, 39.

[432] LeBaron, *Bridging Cultural Conflicts: A New Approach for a Changing World*, 278.

resolution "rituals" such as litigation and interest-based negotiation focus on fair settlements rather than a deep regeneration of the parties and collectivities. Plato's conviction that poetry disguises and distorts reality marked a significant break from oral to written culture in the West and its role in ethics and justice.[433] Losing our oral tradition and embracing rationality, we lost our capacity for regeneration through the spoken word.[434] Repetitive and rhythmic signals generate limbic arousal, bring about a discharge of accumulated pain and deepen integration within the self for both actor and audience.[435] Moreover, they transcend dualism and the experience of unity is born.[436]

There are signs, however, of its gradual re-emergence. In the 1960s, musical protests emerged against the Vietnam War. Today, musical activists weave political themes about the environment, Indigenous rights, feminism, and anti-corporatism into their songs, challenging the hegemony of worldview domination and inspiring a new kind of cultural regeneration, bringing the poet back into politics.[437]

Similarly, community plays, such as Not The Way I Heard It are gaining popularity across Canada. For example, inspired by the Enderby–Splats'in success the Downtown Eastside of Vancouver recently put together a play entitled In The Heart of a City: The Downtown Eastside Community Play (co-produced by Carnegie Community Centre and Vancouver Moving Theatre). They hired four writers representing the various cultural groups in the community and gathered stories from First Nations, Japanese-Canadian, Chinese-Canadian, and

---

[433] Anne Nguyen, "Poetry, Politics, and Government from Plato to the Present," (Victoria: 2001), 15-16.

[434] Ibid.

[435] Richard and Appel Schechner, Willa, ed., By Means of Performance: Intercultural Studies of Theatre and Ritual (Cambridge: Cambridge University Press, 1990), 38-39.

[436] Ibid., 39.

[437] Nguyen, "Poetry, Politics, and Government from Plato to the Present," 1.

Euro-Canadian community members. They wove stories from the various cultural groups spanning the last one hundred and fifty years into the play. Over eighty community members acted in the play walking together through their common and sometimes divergent history in colourful costumes and with giant puppets. In many ways, theatre such as this has a ritualistic quality in that it builds community cohesion, evokes a healing spirit, and creates a kind of liminal space between the past, present and future.[438]

In summary, regenerating cultures and collectivities is best fostered through ritualising transitions, celebrating resiliency, grieving losses, being with the unknown without rushing to either cling to the past or grasp for the future, and nurturing imagination to allow the new creation to come forth. John Paul Lederach challenges us to live not "by the way things are but according to a vision of things not seen. That vision of things not seen eventually changes the way things are."[439] Dreamers, he claims, are essential for movement towards reconciliation. He challenges us "to stay so close to the ground that we feel the very soil's moisture bubbling up from people's daily life, pains, and realities. Yet we must be so close to our dreams of what could be that we can feel and hear the seeds pregnant with life as they break forth from below the surface."[440]

Indeed, Ernie Crey does just that:

> *The day will soon come when First Nations people and whites[441] will sit together to take part in the greatest potlatch of all. They will talk and sing about the wonderful world they will be leaving for their children.*[442]

---

[438] Schechner, ed., *By Means of Performance: Intercultural Studies of Theatre and Ritual*, 19-24.

[439] Lederach, *The Journey Toward Reconciliation*, 197.

[440] Ibid.

[441] I would add all newcomers to this land.

[442] Ernie Crey, "The Children of Tommorrow's Great Potlatch," *BC Studies Journal* 89 (1991): 158.

PART THREE

The Way Out

CHAPTER 5

THE STONE IN YOUR SHOE

It isn't the mountain ahead that wears you out,
but it's the grain of sand in your shoe.[443]

In this final chapter, I would like to paint, with some broad strokes, a picture of where worldviewing skills fit within the bigger picture. In addition, I offer some suggestions for the personal work involved in learning these skills.

First, it can be helpful to see the distance we have traveled since the beginning of the book. In Part One, **The Way In**, I describe a new definition and framework for reconciliation. I offer the following four guiding touchstones for personal and political transformation:

- Drawing on the worldviews of the parties
- Transcending the victim-offender cycle
- Engaging in large-scale social change
- Assessing timing and tactics

---

[443]Robert Service, ([cited December 10 2003]); available from www.cyber-nation.com/victory/quotations/authors/quotes-service_robertw.html.

Each touchstone draws its nourishment from worldviews, leading the way to the critical importance worldviewing skills play for transformation in our relationships, our communities, our cultures, and ourselves.

In Part Two, **Worldviewing Skills**, I use storytelling as a vehicle to illustrate three distinct worldviewing skill sets. *The Singing Mediator* demonstrates how drawing on the worldviews of the parties themselves breathes new meaning into conflicts and their resolutions, helping parties transcend victim-offender cycles and live up to their highest ideals. In *When Worlds Collide*, I tease out practical skills for when our code of ethics is violated and how to build mutual relationships across worldview differences. Finally, in *Out of The Ashes, Phoenix Rises*, I draw on stories of regeneration in both Indigenous and Western cultures and the interdependence of both.

Now, in Part Three, **The Way Out**, I would like to locate worldviewing skills in the bigger picture as well as give a thumbnail sketch of the personal work needed to contribute to the genesis of a new era.

Rising and Falling

Throughout time and around the world there has been a common thread of the rising and falling of civilizations, eras and cultures. From the fall of the Roman Empire to the current downward spiral in many parts of the world, what is common is the paradox of change and unity co-existing despite appearances to the contrary. While on the surface there is turmoil, conflict, and broken relationships, on a deeper level there is also an order and unity that eventually emerges.

The Earth is also in a constant process of change while maintaining its unity. When one species becomes extinct, another species is born; when ice melts, land may become ocean. Conversely, when ice forms a continent may be born. We are not victims of environmental change or disasters but rather participants in a larger community that stretches out beyond our own planet and even our galaxy. Our participation requires the humility to see ourselves as part of a much bigger picture. When we do so, we see more clearly our responsibility to take our lives seriously, share our gifts with the world and live in respectful interdependence with the rest of creation.

Out of chaos, order is born. This is a law of the universe and applies equally to the birth and death of stars in the galaxies, the rising and falling of eras, and even the ebb and flow of our own lives.

The global changes that we are currently experiencing are monumental: civilizations and cultures are in the process of disintegration and genesis; the Earth itself is changing; and the reverberation is being experienced within communities, families and in the daily life of every individual.

Arnold Toynbee wrote a masterpiece about the breakdown, disintegration, and genesis of civilizations from the beginning of recorded history and around the world. He explains that during the disintegration phase of a civilization, violence increases and people respond with less creativity and more rigidity to stress, conflict and change.

Toynbee explains that the genesis of civilizations throughout time have always started with a creative minority, individuals who have experienced profound spiritual transformations and retreated temporarily from their communities. When they return to society, they bring with them a new way of living in the world. In essence they become the spark for a new era. The question becomes how can each one of us become this spark?

Personal Work

The birth of a new era calls for creativity and the capacity to be with the unknown. Trying to fix what is disintegrating can sometimes lead to decay and judgment. Just as propping up the Roman Empire was futile, trying to fix a depression prematurely may abort the discovery of its gifts. It is important to remember that within chaos are the seeds of order; and from death, new life often emerges.

Each of us has a unique life journey and a tapestry of experiences. We have all felt profound pain and loss. At one time or another we have been disappointed, hurt, and felt sorrow. Everyone has also experienced moments of joy and connectedness.

The challenge is to transcend our life story, so that hurtful events of the past do not dictate our actions and are not recreated in the present or our future. The most valuable contribution we can make to the world is to clean up our own backyards and be the catalyst for a new emerging era.

The following is a brief overview of some of the key skills I have found useful in my own life as well as from working with people from around the world.

1. Purpose

Transforming pain into purpose is one of the most effective ways to transcend victimization and find the fuel for living our lives fully.

Some examples:

- A woman loses two children to suicide and becomes a motivational speaker on how to live life everyday despite the grief.

- A girl grows up in a concentration camp and later lives with post-traumatic stress disorder for decades until one day she slowly begins to unearth the gifts she learned about life from living in the camp. She eventually decides to share with other survivors the gifts she discovered that lay hidden in the pain.

2. Root It Out

We have all experienced pain early in life, in one form or another. These experiences can be like seeds.

Although the person is no longer there or the event is long over, the message that we received can take root and take on a life of its own, often dictating our actions even decades later. We need to take responsibility for our lives and root out these messages.

Some examples:

- A child is told repeatedly that she is ugly. As an adult, she believes this to be true. She decides to root out this belief by acknowledging the source of her belief, gaining the cooperation of her inner critic, and intentionally noticing her own beauty.

- A boy is slapped on the head at school and told he is stupid. Even though later in life he becomes very successful, he still believes this to be true and feels worthless deep inside. Once he faces his pain, grieves lost opportunities, and develops self-worth, suddenly his most intimate relationships improve.

3. Mirrors

Often we are unaware of our own inner critics or disavowed parts. The best way to discover them is to notice when we are irritated, judge others, and experience hatred or repulsion. The people we judge or even hate can become powerful mirrors reflecting the very parts of ourselves we dislike, allowing us to transform our own self-hate into acceptance.

Some examples:

- A woman is furious at her spouse for bossing her around while organizing a large family gathering. He has taken over every detail and overrides her own preferences even though this is an important event for her. As she vents her frustration to her friend, she suddenly realizes that she tends to boss others around, and develops a new awareness of her own behaviour and now works to temper it.

- A francophone man discovers that his anger at Indigenous people was misplaced. He realizes his animosity was a good mirror for his own life. He was not angry at Indigenous people's desire for self-determination, his feelings were rooted in his own desire for self-determination for Quebec. Underneath his anger he discovers a frustration and despair that he felt about achieving self-determination for Quebec in his lifetime. Once he realizes this, he begins to collaborate with Indigenous people for their self-determination as he realizes it was intrinsically linked to his own.

4. Rituals and Symbolic Acts

Some experiences are so painful and unjust that the best way to transcend them is through ritual. Rituals create a safe space to grieve our pain, let go of the past, and commit to live life fully. Rituals can also help us reveal the gifts hidden in our pain.

Some examples:

- A boy who was abused incessantly by his uncle decides to build a fire. As he watches the flame, he grieves his experience, letting the tears fall until he has shed his last tear. When the fire is out, he takes the ashes and commits to taking the gift of discernment from his experience and later he works to protect others.

- Four women decide to have a ritual in the woods to ground themselves in nature and to express all of who they are. They develop the ritual as they go along depending on the needs in the moment. They incorporate fire, drumming, storytelling, and time by themselves in nature. One woman describes the ritual as profoundly healing. Showing who she is, fully and genuinely in the context of unconditional acceptance, gives her a new sense of confidence, transforms her relationship to food (which previously had been difficult), and results in a deeper connection to others and to nature.

5. Intimacy with the Earth

All great new ideas that have led to cultural revolutions have started with observing the Earth. For example, Copernicus' assertion that the Earth revolves around the sun led not only to a scientific breakthrough but also started a cultural revolution in how people viewed themselves and the universe.

Observing nature and developing an intimacy with our environment also fosters personal transformation, leaps in consciousness and the birth of new ideas. Every moment is full of meaning, if we only pay attention.

Some examples:

- A survivor of residential school who used alcohol to numb the pain of his memories recounts his own turning point, when one day he woke up from a drunken stupor and saw the whole universe and his own place within the cosmos. He then heard a voice that told him he belongs in this wide web of creation. Since that day, he stopped drinking alcohol and instead has faced his pain. He is now a

force for healing and reconciliation for his community and nation.

❋ A woman has a problem with a colleague, so she
asks the world for help. As soon as she asks, an
eagle swoops down beside her onto the water and
flaps its wings. She takes it as a sign to do something surprising and playful with her colleague.
She does so and discovers an immediate shift in the
relationship, previously riddled with animosity, but
now there are seeds of mutual appreciation.

Life is like a long journey up a mountain, we all have great
challenges to overcome as well as adventures along the way.
Whether it is the loss of a loved one, experiences of abuse or
humiliation, betrayal, or abandonment each one of us has a
mountain to climb.

These experiences can be the fuel to propel us forward giving a larger purpose to our pain. They can also be a burden,
holding us back as we re-create the past in the present or do
not live our lives fully because of the grief or fear we hold
inside.

In this very moment, I feel a deep grief. It is a grief I have
worked with my whole life. At times it burbles up unexpect-
edly and sometimes I would rather it didn't. What I have
learned is that in the midst of grief, something else begins to
arise, an unexpected optimism for my life and others. Para-
doxically, this grief also gives me strength to go on. In this
work of worldviewing, we touch grief and we carry on. We
don't let it discourage us or paralyse us, but rather we use it
as a gift to propel us forward.

No matter how committed we are to social change, justice,
and ultimately reconciliation, if we don't do our personal
work we will likely, despite our best intentions, contribute to
the problems we seek to change. While a conflict with a
neighbour or dealing with the pain of our past may seem
insignificant in comparison to resolving historical and con-

temporary injustices, it is precisely "these stones in our shoe" that ultimately prevents many peace-building strategies from reaching the goals many of us strive for.

We need to start with who we are, what our personal history and legacy is, and how we contribute to conflict or reconciliation in our moment-by-moment choices. It is in the juice of our interactions with others – be it a baker, a colleague, a grocer, or our partner that we can learn these skills. Our challenge is where and how we meet the Other. When we use worldviewing skills, what arises is a great sense of respect because on some level the Other provides an opportunity to either climb our mountain or become stagnant.

When we transform our pain into purpose, turn enemies into friends, develop an intimacy with nature, and share our gifts with the world then we will know we are the spark for a new era rising out of the ashes.

APPENDIX I

METHODOLOGY

We cannot discover new oceans unless we
have the courage to lose sight of the shore.[444]

Reconciliation is certainly a journey, even as one writes a book on the topic. In what follows I first describe why I entered Graduate school. Next, I describe my path through various experiences and literature that brought me to the field of reconciliation and, eventually, to the working definition I suggest and the four guiding touchstones I propose. Third, I lay out my methodological praxis. Fourth, I explain my rationale for exploring in greater detail the role worldviews play in creating conditions for meaningful reconciliation. Finally, I end by describing the various ways my methodological praxis deepened in direct relation to my own expanding consciousness and praxis.

Motivation

In 2000, I worked briefly for a Peruvian human rights organization during the period prior to the ousting of President Fujimori. As in many contexts prior to large-scale social change, repression was particularly high. On the eve of my first day of work, a journalist who was trying to expose various aspects of government corruption was severely tortured and nearly died. While my colleagues went to the hospital to offer legal and psychological counsel, I translated details of

---

[444] Anonymous in Danaan Parry, *Warriors of the Heart* (Bainbridge Island: The Earthstewards Network, 1991), 85.

the torture case for international diffusion. I soon discovered a fraudulent election process, death threats, torture, and random acts of violence were strategies frequently used by the Fujimori regime to hold on to power and repress any attempts for social change. As repression increased, I became increasingly concerned about my own safety and began to ask questions about the risks involved in the work I was doing. I soon discovered that most people did not want to even broach the subject. I realized that in order to survive, there was a kind of collective denial about the dangers involved in working for social change at that time.

On my return to Canada, I realized that every context has its own version of collective denial and became interested in how it manifested with regards to Indigenous and non-Indigenous relations in this land. Moreover, as I looked at my own context and around the world, I felt that both violent conflict and environmental devastation were likely to worsen. Given that both were human-made disasters, I felt the solution lay in better understanding the nature of collective denial and learning ways to shift collective consciousness.

I realized that if I were to make any serious contributions to the world I would need time to think, as most efforts towards social change seemed to create more problems than offer any significant solution. The only way I knew how to take the time I needed to think without working was to go to Graduate school. Dr. Taiaiake Alfred, who had been my undergraduate advisor at Concordia University, had in the meantime become the Director of Indigenous Governance at the University of Victoria. I therefore asked for his advice regarding Graduate programs and pursued his recommendation to come to the University of Victoria.

Choosing a Research Topic

Initially, I was drawn to restorative justice and truth commissions as they seemed to address some important elements I was seeking when thinking about societal transformation –

namely denial, accountability, and healing. I therefore chose research topics related to truth commissions and restorative justice for the first two semesters of my Graduate program. An important turning point in my inquiry was working as a facilitator at a three-week healing retreat for First Nations women survivors of residential schools. The experience helped me understand intergenerational trauma better, the nature of victim-offender cycles, and most importantly the large gap in terms of non-Indigenous rehabilitation and accountability in righting our relationships. Through a restorative justice lens, it seemed to me that Indigenous people were doing their part of the work necessary to transform our relationship – namely healing, cultural regeneration, economic sustainability, and political consciousness raising. I became acutely aware that there was a tremendous amount of work yet to be done on the non-Indigenous side of our relationship – such as transcending collective denial, fostering collective responsibility, and learning how to build relationships of mutuality.

Around this time, I read an article by Oscar Nudler, an Argentinean worldview conflict theorist, entitled *On Conflicts and Metaphors*.[445] Nudler describes the role worldviews play in human survival and argues that the imposition of one worldview on another is an extreme form of oppression, worse than purely economic exploitation. Reading his article was like coming out of a fog. I began to see more clearly how many of our strategies to resolve Indigenous – non-Indigenous conflicts were rooted in a Euro-Canadian worldview and therefore did nothing to transform the heart of our relationship – namely worldview domination. Moreover, seeing our joint histories through a worldview lens helped me better appreciate the level of trauma inflicted on Indigenous people and gave me a hint on how to shift non-Indigenous consciousness.

---

[445] Oscar Nudler, "On Conflicts and Metaphors," in *Conflict Human Needs Theory*, ed. John Burton (London: MacMillan Press, 1990).

I began to see restorative justice and truth commissions as useful only if they are rooted in the culture of the people themselves and are accompanied by structural change. Otherwise it seemed that these strategies were merely indigenised processes without addressing genuine self-determination or understanding the root problem of worldview domination.[446] As I began to realize the limitations of both restorative justice and truth commissions, I realized that to shift relationships from worldview domination to mutuality, it would be more useful to think about capacities within the traditions of the parties themselves that could be useful in fostering reconciliation. I therefore decided to shift my inquiry to the larger goal of reconciliation with an understanding that each culture has its unique pathway to achieve this end result.

Engaged Participation

Being an experiential learner, I decided to broaden my exposure to reconciliation scholarship and practice. The following outlines the various conferences and international academic programs that I attended as well as some of my key learning points that accompanied them.

At Eastern Mennonite University's Conflict Transformation Program, I studied Philosophy and Praxis of Reconciliation with Dr. Hizkias Assefa (May 2002), Victim-Offender Mediation of Violent Crimes with Dave Guftasen and Sandy Bergen (May 2002), and Fundamentals in Peace-building with Dr. John Paul Lederach (January 2003). In addition to learning from such skilled practitioners and scholars, I studied and lived with a variety of people from around the world working towards reconciliation in their own contexts. In this way, I was able to learn first hand about countries such as Fiji,

---

[446] For a more detailed analysis see Jessie Sutherland, *Colonialism, Crime, and Dispute Resolution: A Critical Analysis of Canada's Aboriginal Justice Strategy* (2002 [cited December 10 2003]); available from http://work.acresolution.org/research.nsf/key/BoskeyGradWinner2002.

East Timor, Nagaland, Bosnia, Rwanda, Congo, Sierra Leone, and Liberia. This experience convinced me that reconciliation was indeed the thesis topic I wanted to explore. I realized it offered not just another conflict handling approach but rather a paradigm shift that involved the following four dimensions to righting our relationships: self, others, nature, and spirituality.[447]

Next, I attended the Caux Scholars program in Switzerland which offers twenty students from around the world an opportunity to live and study together on topics such as reconciliation, trauma healing, early warning and conflict prevention, and the impact the "war on terrorism" has on liberations struggles worldwide. In addition to the course work, students attended many international conferences that were in progress in the same centre. In fact, for the Agenda for Reconciliation conference we were assigned various delegations to accompany. I accompanied the Sierra Leonean delegation, made up of an ex-rebel leader, the Minister of Interior Affairs, and various non-governmental representatives. I witnessed first hand apology, acceptance, and forgiveness between the ex-rebel leader and the Minister of Interior Affairs who just two years before had been deadly enemies.

In addition to these academic programs I attended several conferences and workshops to gain a better understanding of reconciliation within the Canadian context. I attended *A Just and Lasting Reconciliation: First Nations Government* in Vancouver (March 2002), a First Nations elders conference on *Spiritual Unity* in the Tsartlipp community (July 2002), *Pilgrimage Towards Right Relationships* gathering at the United Church in Parkville (April 2003), the Dispute Resolution Symposium in Vancouver (April 2003), a community play entitled *In The Heart of City: The Downtown Eastside Community Play*, which weaves the stories of the various cultural groups in Vancou-

---

[447] Hizkias Assefa, "Peace and Reconciliation as a Paradigm: A Philosophy of Peace and Its Implications on Conflict, Governance and Economic Growth," (Nairobi: 2001), 10-13.

ver's downtown eastside over the past one hundred and fifty years (November 2003), and an Anglican church's weekly lecture series comparing early Celtic spirituality to that of First Nations' as well as their similar experience with colonialism (November 2003). From these events, I learned about various initiatives and strategies within First Nations communities, the Canadian government, and grassroots leadership.

Reconciliation and The Four Guiding Touchstones

In addition to the experiential learning mentioned above, I did an interdisciplinary literature review which drew on the following fields: conflict resolution, conflict transformation, restorative justice, transitional justice, peace-building, international relations, critical legal theory, Indigenous political movements, intercultural studies, anthropology, psychology, and trauma healing. Thus I read many books, articles, and the texts of speeches related to large-scale reconciliation.

Although the material was disparate as well as voluminous, Dr. Antoinette Oberg guided me through a self-reflective process that helped me develop a focus for both the content and methodology of my thesis. With the help of Dr. Oberg's insights, I developed a working definition for reconciliation and identified four guiding touchstones that can help create conditions for reconciliation. Consequently, in this book, reconciliation refers to the parallel process of personal and political transformation from systems of domination to relationships of mutuality. I propose the following four guiding touchstones: drawing on the fundamental worldviews of the parties themselves, transcending the victim-offender cycle, engaging in large-scale social change, and assessing timing and tactics.

Methodology as Praxis

Initially, I intended to write a thesis describing these four touchstones and then using them to evaluate the current residential school alternative dispute resolution process in Canada. However, it soon became clear that, given the nature of reconciliation, its newness to academic research, and my own shifts in understanding, an emergent design would be more appropriate. Richard Tarnas explains that cognition and intellectual imagination are directly interdependent with a developed inner life and an ever-emerging consciousness.[448] In this way, an emergent design enabled me to deepen my methodology in direct relationship to my own ever-emerging consciousness as described below.

Initially, I drew on critical social theory to describe the four touchstones. As I got further into my work I realized my writing was incongruent with my main argument. For example, I wrote about the importance of developing "worldviewing skills" yet only wrote from one worldview, namely a traditional linear and theoretical academic style. This approach was antithetical to "worldviewing skills" which emphasizes the use of storytelling, metaphors, and legends as a way to breathe meaning and life into words and actions. Furthermore, I realized that by using critical social theory I was inadvertently contributing to a victim-offender paradigm, while at the same time I was advocating the need to transcend this very dynamic. Moreover, in writing a traditional academic paper for an academic audience I was contributing to the practitioner-academic gap. Consequently, I was not building relationships with unlike-minded and unlike-situated people, a necessary pre-condition for building a large-scale social change movement for reconciliation. Finally, by trying to tackle all touchstones I was not modelling timing and tactics. In attempting to give a comprehensive description and application of each touchstone, I was not starting with where things were, but rather where I hoped them to be.[449]

This awareness led me to realize that, despite my best efforts, I too had internalised the very attitudes and practices

---

[448] Richard Tarnas, *The Passion of the Western Mind: Understanding the Ideas That Have Shaped Our World View* (New York: Harmony Books, 1991), 434.

[449] Saul Alinsky, *Rules for Radicals: A Pragmatic Primer for Realistic Radicals* (New York: Vintage, 1971), xix.

that are imbedded in systems of domination. I understood that, regardless of our intentions or positions in society, we all internalize to varying degrees many of the elements we wish to change and inadvertently contribute to the very conflicts we seek to resolve. In this way, I decided it was not accurate to talk about reconciliation as something to only do to others, but as a paradigm rooted first within one's self. I soon discovered that while many peace-building and reconciliation literature espouse the necessity for practitioners to "embody peace," there is actually very little written about what that entails. Consequently, it seemed more appropriate to discuss the touchstones as a set of skills and knowledge that anyone who is interested in creating conditions for reconciliation can learn.

This new awareness led me to a methodological dilemma. Given that many methodologies are embedded in the very paradigm that I was seeking to change, I was at a loss for how to proceed. As Richard Tarnas explains,

> *The pursuit of knowledge always takes place within a given paradigm, within a conceptual matrix – a womb that provides an intellectually nourishing structure, that fosters growth and increasing complexity and sophistication – until gradually that structure is experienced as constricting, a limitation, a prison, producing a tension of irresolvable contradictions, and finally a crisis is reached. Then some inspired Promethean genius comes along and is graced with an inner breakthrough to a new vision that gives the scientific mind a new sense of cognitively connected-reconnected to the world: an intellectual revolution occurs, and a new paradigm is born.*

Again, Dr. Antoinette Oberg became my Promethean[450] genius. She introduced me to Patty Lather's article "Research

---

[450] In Greek mythology Prometheus stole the fire from the heavens and gave it to humans. He symbolizes the emergence of the "rational man" from a more primitive state. See Tarnas, *The Passion of the Western Mind: Understanding the Ideas That Have Shaped Our World View*, 14.

as Praxis", where she describes how new paradigm inquiry requires aligning your methodology with your research topic as a way to produce "emancipatory knowledge."[451] I therefore decided that my methodology needed to be congruent with the skills I was advocating. Consequently, I chose to use the four guiding touchstones as my methodology

In this way, I felt I would simultaneously develop these skills personally and model them in my writing. The following describes each touchstone and how it relates to my research methodology:

1. Drawing on the worldviews of the parties themselves

I endeavoured to write in a way that reflected the world-viewing skills I described. For example, given that metaphors are windows into a culture's worldview,[452] I described various aspects of culture and the role of worldviews in human survival through the use of a variety of metaphors such as "a fish in water", the "iceberg analogy," the "tree analogy," and the gestalt ambiguous figure. Moreover, since I am suggesting that one of the root causes of deep-rooted conflict is the loss of meaning and hence the disconnection from our relationship to the rest of the universe, I used as many analogies connected to the Earth as possible. In this way, I hoped to encourage symbolic literacy[453] – a pre-requisite for re-thinking how best to organize human affairs given our current knowledge about the nature of the world.

In addition, I decided to weave legends, stories, narratives, and theory together as a way to reflect good worldviewing

---

[451] Patty Lather, "Research as Praxis," *Harvard Educational Review* 56, no. 3 (1986): 259.

[452] LeBaron, *Bridging Cultural Conflicts: A New Approach for a Changing World*, 283.

[453] Robert Vachon and Raimon Panikkar suggests symbolic illiteracy is more of a problem than functional illiteracy. See Vachon, "Guswenta or the Intercultural Imperative: Towards a Re-Enacted Peace Accord between the Mohawk Nation and the North American Nation-States (and Their People)," 45.

skills that value multiple ways of seeing and knowing. I did this by first listing on large poster paper all the worldview conflict theory I hoped to cover in this book. Next I considered what stories, metaphors, or legends I could use to tease out the various worldview theories I hoped to incorporate. In this way I was able to divide the application part of this book into three worldviewing skill sets: connecting parties' to their fundamental worldview, skills to bridge worldview difference, and the regeneration of cultures.

Moreover, as I deepened my understanding between the global loss of meaning, violence in the world today, and the need for cultural regeneration to foster reconciliation, I also deepened my methodology to reflect this awareness. Consequently, each set of worldviewing skills that I describe reflects key elements for the regeneration of cultures: living our values and storytelling.

Further, whenever I had a writing block, I drew on worldviewing skills by engaging in "metaphor journeying."[454] For example, when it came to writing the chapter about the regeneration of cultures, I drew a blank on how best to proceed. First, I turned to Rigoberta Menchu's words when she said, "you may have taken the foliage and branches and even the trunk of our tradition, but we still have our roots." [455] This led me to consider what conditions foster growth after a forest fire. Asking a friend who knows a great deal about reforestation, I discovered that pine forests require extreme heat for pinecones to germinate and hence produce a stronger and

---

[454] Oscar Nudler developed "metaphor dialoguing" as a way for conflicting parties with different worldviews to explore solutions. Michelle LeBaron refers to this technique as metaphor journeying and expands its use to problem-solving and conflict resolution (see 2003, 260-267). I found it extremely useful in overcoming 'concept blocks' when writing and researching.

[455] G Esteva, "Enough, Basta," The Ecologist 24, no. 3 (1994): 84 in, Vachon, "Guswenta or the Intercultural Imperative: Towards a Re-Enacted Peace Accord between the Mohawk Nation and the North American Nation-States (and Their People)."

more resilient forest. Exploring this metaphor further, I wondered if there could be any equivalent for cultural regeneration. Quickly, my friend suggested the Legend of the Phoenix,[456] where the bird must first die onto itself before it can rise out of the ashes. I soon discovered the Cherokee named one of their newspapers, *The Cherokee Phoenix*, after this mythical bird as a symbol of regeneration following *The Trail of Tears*.[457] After carefully reading the Legend of the Phoenix (see Appendix III), I discovered many of the key elements necessary for cultural regeneration: ritualising transitions, celebrating one's life, relaxing into the unknown or the void, and grieving loses before the new life can take flight.

2. Transcending the victim-offender paradigm

Conscious of the various roles (such as victim, offender, accomplice, bystander, and rescuer) that keep systems of domination in place and fuel victim – offender dynamics, I endeavoured to transcend this dynamic within my methodology. First, I decided not to judge any author but rather to focus on how to create conditions that foster genuine reconciliation. Second, throughout this book I strove to reinforce qualities such as self-responsibility, openness, and power based on personal integrity rather than coercive force. Third, I considered the important role the limbic adrenal gland plays in victim-offender cycles. Consequently, I chose stroytelling as a framework for describing deep-rooted conflict because new brain research links this art form to meaning-making and it even has the capacity to reverse our "fight or flight" tendencies. In this way, I hoped to transcend in my methodology the victim-offender paradigm discussed in this touchstone.

---

[456]See Appendix IV.

[457]In 1838, the Cherokee were forcibly removed from their territories. This event is known as "The Trail of Tears."

3. Engaging in large-scale social change

Touchstone Three argues that reconciliation involves a large-scale social change process that endeavours to weave webs of relationships across difference. Consequently, I wove narratives with theory as a way to bridge the practitioner-researcher gap. Similarly, by avoiding academic language, I strove to write in a way that would be accessible to everyone.

Moreover, as I wrote I attended many events related to reconciliation that reflected a wide spectrum of perspectives cutting across all sectors of society. While I do not refer directly to the many conversations or correspondence connected with the various relationships I developed over the course of its writing, they nonetheless influenced the final content. For example, when I received emails from friends working on peace-building in areas where they lost over one hundred people in their own village to a rebel group or others who risked their lives to meet with rebel leaders in the bush I was reminded of the very real consequences of the dynamics I was writing about. In this way, I was constantly brought back to the urgency of the issues I wrote about.

These relationships helped me focus my research with the hopes to produce something that would be useful to real people working on deep-rooted conflict. Consequently, I strove to draw on personal, interpersonal, intra-community, inter-community, intra-state, and inter-state initiatives to foster reconciliation.

4. Timing and Tactics

As I prepared for presenting at a conference in Switzerland with three colleagues, I was challenged in deciding just what of my research I would present in the allocated fifteen minutes. Eventually, I settled on worldviewing skills as they relate to reconciliation. Because conference participants came from approximately eighty countries, and included grassroots non-governmental activists, academics, and senior government leaders, I had to select an approach meaningful to everyone. I therefore decided to use my experience as a group leader for a Cree-francophone youth exchange to tease out various worldviewing skills and then show their implications for the larger international human security and peace-building agenda of regenerating cultural pluralism.

Our contribution appeared to have a major impact on the conference. After my talk several people approached me to discuss the implications of what I was talking about in their own context. An Ethiopian law student graduating from Oxford, realized his studies were incongruent with notions of justice and governance in his own context and began to consider how to regenerate more meaningful institutions in Ethiopia. A political science masters student from Sierra Leone realized his thesis topic, regional African organizations, was based on Western models and began to question how to develop African organizations that were African in character. An Eastern European woman began to question her own beliefs and wondered how to maintain a different worldview in the face of worldview hegemony. In addition, the term "worldviewing skills" was frequently referred to throughout the remaining days of the conference. For example, when a significant difference emerged in conversations, people said, "I think we need some worldviewing skills." Moreover, "worldviewing skills" were often referred to in plenary summaries of the day's events. In this way, "worldviewing skills" as a concept and praxis shifted the discussion from fixing problems in the world to developing mutually reciprocal relationships and regenerating worldview pluralism.

In addition, my colleague Mary Alice Smith (Métis) and I facilitated a workshop entitled *Weaving Worldwide Webs For Reconciliation*. Drawing on John Paul Lederach's "web out" approach (Touchstone Three), we facilitated an interactive workshop where participants had an opportunity to begin to think strategically about building a large-scale reconciliation movement in their own context. Through this experience I realized how the "web out" approach could potentially add fuel to already volatile conflicts if the practitioners themselves had not already learned worldviewing skills and developed capacities to transcend the victim-offender cycle. It became clear to me that an effective large-scale social change movement for reconciliation must begin with the consciousness of the individual, including peace-building practitioners themselves.

The following day, my colleagues Dorothy Christian from the Shuswap and Okanagan First Nations and Victoria Freeman, a Euro-Canadian, presented their personal journeys on the panel, *Understanding the Other*. Their speeches were personal and very powerful. In fact, the entire dynamic of the conference shifted after their presentation. Rather than discussing how to solve African problems, many Europeans and Africans began to discuss their colonial relationships and the impact it had on how they worked together today. There was a deepening of authentic conversation and a willingness to face the heart of the problem. Many conference participants were inspired in a new way to tackle their most difficult problems and frequently told me that they had often heard First Nations give talks or Euro-Canadians present but had never witnessed a joint effort to talk about the heart of our relationship.

Presenting together at this conference had a significant impact on the focus as well as the timing and tactics of this book. I remembered earlier conversations about worldviews and their regenerative effects. For example, at the First Nations reconciliation conference in Vancouver, Leah Whiu, a Maori scholar from the University of Waikato in New Zealand and I discussed in hushed voices collective denial, strategies to shift collective consciousness, and the dissonance between social change strategies and the cultures of the Indigenous people. As we shared on a more personal level, our insights deepened, and we realized how the set up of the conference itself ran counter to regenerating Indigenous cultures and fostering dialogue amongst equals. For example, many of the panel discussions were typical question and answer format and the location was at an expensive downtown Vancouver hotel far removed from Indigenous communities and grassroots initiatives. What struck me the most about this conversation was its immediate impact. Leah Whiu was one of the first speakers that morning and, rather than presenting her prepared speech, she stood at the back of the room and sang a Maori song. She followed the song with a speech that came directly from the heart about the importance of starting first with oneself. In turn, she set an important tone for the remaining speakers and the atmosphere was alive with energy and possibility.

I realized one of the biggest obstacles in transforming systems of domination to relationships of mutuality is worldview domination, yet it is frequently the most overlooked aspect. The experience at the conference in Switzerland helped me realize that if I were to start with where things were rather than where I would like them to be, I would need to focus in greater detail on worldviewing skills. Given my new focus, my research question became "What role do worldviews play to foster meaningful reconciliation?" Thus I hypothesize that worldviewing skills are central to and provide the necessary foundation for lasting and meaningful reconciliation.

In choosing the sequencing of chapters illustrating worldviewing skills, I drew on Milton Bennett's article, *Towards Ethnorelativism: A Developmental Model of Intercultural Sensitivity*, which outlines how to facilitate intercultural learning and skill development. Consequently, each chapter builds on the knowledge base of the previous chapter. After laying the foundation with a comprehensive literature review, I chose the following three main worldview skill sets for more detailed analysis: connecting parties to their fundamental worldview, skills for when worldviews collide, and finally regenerating damaged or distorted worldviews.

This sequence also reflects my argument that violence today is not related to a "clash of civilizations" but rather to a mutual "collapse of civilizations." Since we are now coming to the end of the Enlightenment era, one based on rational thought, I begin this book with a rational framework of a comprehensive literature review. I then progressively introduce concepts that reflect more of symbolic frames of reference. What I intend to model is not that we are necessarily going from one paradigm to another so much as coming to a synthesis of paradigms that value rationalism, symbolism, and other ways of knowing.

Mats Alvesson and Kaj Skolberg explain that creative processes emerge from the fusion of "seemingly disparate phenomena"[458] Indeed, I discovered that as I wrote in ways whereby polar opposites co-existed, such as by weaving stories and theory from disparate fields together, there was a creative tension that often produced new insights. For example in using a tree as a metaphor to describe the importance of cultural consistency and exploring Indigenous loss of meaning, I realized that Western culture was facing a similar crisis, leading me to investigate Western political theory, theology, new sciences, cosmology, consciousness, anthropology, and chaos theory. As I wove information from more disciplines into the framework of storytelling I continually came to a greater synthesis and understanding reflecting one of my main arguments about the opportunities worldview differences present: deepening our own cultural roots and broadening our understanding about life itself.

Given that this book's methodology is based on new-paradigm research, I was faced with various ethical dilemmas. For example, since reconciliation is such a new way of resolving intra-state conflicts, knowledge is continually being created. While the body of this book's content was developed from documentary research, how could I incorporate some of the emerging knowledge and insights not yet documented or fully formed? Moreover, given reconciliation is primarily about relationships of mutuality and that an important

---

[458]Alvesson , Mats and Skoldberg, Kaj. Reflexive Methodology: New Vistas for Qualitative Research (London: Sage Publications, 2000), 251

touchstone involves meaning making, I encountered a further dilemma, how was I going to make meaning out of the variety of stories that I wrote about in a way that honoured worldview pluralism? How could I choose stories that could foster an essential principle of emancipatory research – reciprocity?[459]

I therefore chose published stories that not only illustrate the skills and knowledge necessary for fostering reconciliation, but also stories connected to people whom I knew and could submit my writing to for reciprocal feedback in their meaning and interpretation. For example, Dr. Felix Kaputo, professor of literature, exegesis, and oral history from the University of Lubumbashi in the Republic of Congo and Perry Mbibong, Caux scholar alumni, Cameroon[460]reviewed The Singing Mediator. Similarly, Shuswap filmmaker Dorothy Christian and puppet theatre artist Cathy Stubington reviewed *When Worlds Collide* and *Out of the Ashes, Phoenix Rises.*

In addition, several scholars and practitioners reviewed full or partial drafts of this book. The feedback I received was critical in deepening my analysis as well as confirming my research had strong applicability to the field. For example, Chief Robert Joseph, from the British Columbia Indian Residential Schools Survivors Society, immediately called me after he read my work and told me of the strong applicability this book has for his own work. Similarly, after reading *The Singing Mediator*, Dr. Kaputo commented on the importance my work has in his context and was interested in organizing his own students' work around my findings. He also suggested I read Mircea Eliade's work which led me to explore regenerative rituals in a deeper way and to realize the loss of this capacity in Western culture, thereby

---

[459]Lather, "Research as Praxis," 263.

[460]Sam Doe, Executive Director of the West African Network for Education and Peace was sent the chapter however could not give feedback within the time constraints for this book.

strengthening both *The Singing Mediator* and *Out of the Ashes, Phoenix Rises.*

Finally, throughout this book I occasionally use terms such as "we," "ourselves," or "us." My intention is to include myself along with other human beings in our shared struggles to learn worldviewing skills and create cultures of peace. In this way, I do not hold myself in some place of omniscience but rather acknowledge my own emerging consciousness alongside others. Moreover, I am inviting intimacy with the reader as a way to acknowledge that as human beings, despite or because of our diversity, we share common challenges in learning the skills I describe and regaining the fullness of our humanity.

APPENDIX II

TRAUMA HEALING:
BREAKING THE CYCLE OF VIOLENCE[461]

TRAUMA HEALING JOURNEY: BREAKING THE CYCLE OF VIOLENCE

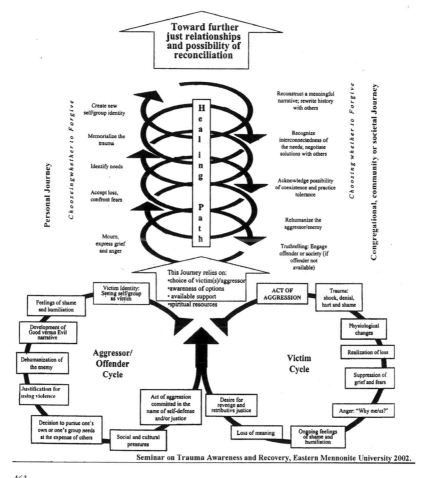

Seminar on Trauma Awareness and Recovery, Eastern Mennonite University 2002.

[461]Reprinted with permission from publisher; See Appendix V.

APPENDIX III

INAC'S (INDIAN AND NORTHERN AFFAIRS CANADA) STATEMENT OF RECONCILIATION[462]

Learning from the Past

As Aboriginal and non-Aboriginal Canadians seek to move forward together in a process of renewal, it is essential that we deal with the legacies of the past affecting the Aboriginal peoples of Canada, including the First Nations, Inuit and Métis. Our purpose is not to rewrite history but, rather, to learn from our past and to find ways to deal with the negative impacts that certain historical decisions continue to have in our society today.

The ancestors of First Nations, Inuit and Métis peoples lived on this continent long before explorers from other continents first came to North America. For thousands of years before this country was founded, they enjoyed their own forms of government. Diverse, vibrant Aboriginal nations had ways of life rooted in fundamental values concerning their relationships to the Creator, the environment, and each other, in the role of Elders as the living memory of their ancestors, and in their responsibilities as custodians of the lands, waters and resources of their homelands.

The assistance and spiritual values of the Aboriginal peoples who welcomed the newcomers to this continent too often have been forgotten. The contributions made by all Aboriginal peoples to Canada's development, and the contributions that they continue to make to our society today, have not been properly acknowledged. The Government of Canada today, on behalf of all Canadians, acknowledges those contributions.

Sadly, our history with respect to the treatment of Aboriginal people is not something in which we can take pride. Attitudes of racial and cultural superiority led to a suppression of Aboriginal culture and values. As a country, we are burdened by past actions that resulted in weakening the identity of Aboriginal peoples, suppressing their languages and cultures, and outlawing spiritual practices. We must recognize the impact of these actions on the once self-sustaining nations that were disaggregated, disrupted, limited or even destroyed by the dispossession of traditional territory, by the relocation of Aboriginal people, and by some provisions of the Indian Act. We must acknowledge that the result of these actions was the erosion of the political, economic and social systems of Aboriginal people and nations.

Against the backdrop of these historical legacies, it is a remarkable tribute to the strength and endurance of Aboriginal people that they have maintained their historic diversity and identity. The Government of Canada today formally expresses to all Aboriginal people in Canada our profound regret for past actions of the federal government which have contributed to these difficult pages in the history of our relationship together.

One aspect of our relationship with Aboriginal people over this period that requires particular attention is the Residential School system. This system separated many children from their families and communities and prevented them from speaking their own languages and from learning about their heritage and cultures. In the worst cases, it left legacies of personal pain and distress that continue to reverberate in Aboriginal communities to this day. Tragically, some children were the victims of physical and sexual abuse.

The Government of Canada acknowledges the role it played in the development and administration of these schools. Particularly to those individuals who experienced the tragedy of sexual and physical abuse at residential schools, and who have carried this burden believing that in some way they must be responsible, we wish to emphasize that what you experienced was not your fault and should never have happened. To those of you who suffered this tragedy at residential schools, we are deeply sorry.

In dealing with the legacies of the Residential School system, the Government of Canada proposes to work with First Nations, Inuit and Métis people, the Churches and other interested parties to resolve the longstanding issues that must be addressed. We need to work together on a healing strategy to assist individuals and communities in dealing with the consequences of this sad era of our history.

No attempt at reconciliation with Aboriginal people can be complete without reference to the sad events culminating in the death of Métis leader Louis Riel. These events cannot be undone; however, we can and will continue to look for ways of affirming the contributions of Métis people in Canada and of reflecting Louis Riel's proper place in Canada's history.

Reconciliation is an ongoing process. In renewing our partnership, we must ensure that the mistakes which marked our past relationship are not repeated. The Government of Canada recognizes that policies that sought to assimilate Aboriginal people, women and men, were not the way to build a strong country. We must instead continue to find ways in which Aboriginal people can participate fully in the economic, political, cultural and social life of Canada in a manner which preserves and enhances the collective identities of Aboriginal communities, and allows them to evolve and flourish in the future. Working together to achieve our shared goals will benefit all Canadians, Aboriginal and non-Aboriginal alike.

APPENDIX IV

THE LEGEND OF THE PHOENIX

The Greek and Roman Phoenix[463]

While the legend of the Phoenix varies slightly from culture to culture the basic premise remains the same. The following is a brief summary followed by a poem by a Roman author, Claudian.[464]

> *The Greek believed that the Phoenix lived in Arabia, in a cool well. At dawn, each morning it sung a beautiful song so beautiful that the Sun god would stop his chariot to listen. The Phoenix is a unique bird, there may only exist one at a time, which makes it a solitary bird. It does not reproduce, which adds to its loneliness, as only its death will bring on another of its race. When it feels its end approaching (between 500 and 1461 years, depending on the legend), it builds a nest with the finest aromatic woods, sets it on fire, and is consumed by his own flames. From the pile of ashes, a new Phoenix arises, young and powerful. It then embalms the ashes of its predecessor in an egg of myrrh, and flies to the city of the Sun, Heliopolis, where he deposits the egg on the altar of the Sun god.*

---

[463]This explanation and poem was excerpted from www.phoenixarises.com/phoenix/legends/greek.htm

[464]Translated by Henry Vaughan

THE PHOENIX

He knows his time is out! and doth provide
New principles of life; herbs he brings dried
From the hot hills, and with rich spices frames
A Pile shall burn, and Hatch him with his flames.

On this the weakling sits; salutes the Sun
With pleasant noise, and prays and begs for some
Of his own fire, that quickly may restore
The youth and vigor, which he had before
Whom Phoebus* spies, stopping his rays

He makes a stand, and thus allays his pains
He shakes his locks, and from his golden head,
Shoots on bright beam, which smiles with vital fire

The willing bird; to burn is his desire.
That he may live again; he's proud in death,
And goes in haste to gain a better breath.
The spice heap fired with celestial rays
Doth burn the aged Phoenix, when straight stays
The Chariot of the amazed Moon; the pole
Resists the wheeling, swift Orbs, and the whole
Fabric of Nature at a stand remains.
Till the old bird anew, young begins again.

APPENDIX V

Copyright permissions and credits

Figure 1: Spectrum of Conflict Handling Mechanisms

Hizkias, Assefa, "The Meaning of Reconciliation," in *People Building Peace: 35 Inspiring stories from around the World,* ed. European Centre for Conflict Prevention (Utrecht: European Centre for Conflict Prevention, 1999), 37.

Reprinted with permission from the author
Hizkias Assefa
PO Box 63560
Nairobi, Kenya

Figure 2: The iceberg analogy

Das in Vachon, "Guswenta or the Intercultural Imperative: Towards a Re-Enacted Peace Accord between the Mohawk Nation and the North American Nation-States (and Their People), 52.

Reprinted with permission from the author
Kalpana Das
Intercultural Institute of Montreal
4917 Rue St. Urbain
Montreal, Quebec H2T 2W1

Figure 3: The tree analogy

Das in Vachon, "Guswenta or the Intercultural Imperative: Towards a Re-Enacted Peace Accord between the Mohawk Nation and the North American Nation-States (and Their People)," 53.

Reprinted with permission from the author:
Kalpana Das
Intercultural Institute of Montreal
4917 Rue St. Urbain
Montreal, Quebec H2T 2W1

Figure 4: The pelican/antelope ambiguous figure

Hanson in Nudler, "On Conflicts and Metaphors," in *Conflict Human Needs Theory*, ed John Burton. London:MacMillan Press, 1990, 198.

Reprinted with permission from the publisher:
Cambridge University Press
40 West 20th Street
New York, NY 10011-4211
USA

Figure 5: The persona, the shadow, and the self

Reprinted with permission from author's
Executor of Estate
Jerilyn Brusseau
Earthstewards Network Publishing Program
PO Box 10697
Bainbridge Island, WA 98110
USA

Figure 6: Four Dimensions of Reconciliation

Permission to reprint these images was granted
by the author:
Hizkias Assefa
PO Box
Nairobi, Kenya

Figure 7: Trauma Healing Journey: Breaking the Cycle of Violence

Reprinted with permission from the publisher
Seminar on Trauma Awareness and Recovery
Eastern Mennonite University
Harrisonburg VA 22802-2462
USA

Photo credits:

Bookcover

Seashell Spiral courtesy of Paul Docherty

Chapter One

Four Touchstones painted by Bonnie Spencer
Rock garden with touchstones photograph by
Hilary Percy
Individual Touchstone photographs by Sylvan Mably

Chapter Two

Griot
Photograph courtesy of Samuel Gaze
(www.agadez-niger.com)

Chapter Three

Not The Way I Heard It Community Play
Photographs courtesy of the Enderby & District Museum.

Chapter Four

National Day Of Healing and Reconciliation Victoria, BC
2005 (see www.ndhr.ca for more information about this
important day)
Photograph by Heidi Lesueur

Chapter Five

Mountain
Photograph by Lois Gardner

BIBLIOGRAPHY

Abram, David. *The Spell of the Sensuous*. New York: Vintage Books, 1996.

Abu-Nimer, Mohammed. "Conflict Resolution Approaches: Western and Middle Eastern Lessons and Possibilities." *American Journal of Economics and Sociology 55:35-52* 55 (1996): 35-52.

———, ed. *Reconciliation, Justice, and Coexistence*. Lanham: Lexington Books, 2001.

Ackerman, Alice. "Reconciliation as a Peace-Building Process in Postwar Europe." *Peace and Change, A Journal of Peace Research* 19, no. 3 (July 1994): 229-50.

Ackerman, Peter; Duval, Jack. *A Force More Powerful: A Century of Nonviolent Conflict*. New York: Palgrave, 2000.

Action, Moveon.org: Democracy in. *Global Candlelight Vigil for Peace*. 2003 [cited 19 March 2003]. Available from http:www.moveon.org/vigil/.

Alfred, Taiaiake. Public lecture, Camosun College, March 18th 2002.

———. Personal communication, January 14 2002.

———. *Deconstructing the British Columbia Treaty Process* 2000 [cited November 15 2003]. Available from http://taiaiake.com/words/.

———. *The First Steps to Freedom* 2002 [cited July 11 2002]. Available from www.taiaiake.com/home/index.html.

———. *My Grandmother, She Raised Me up Again* 2003 [cited April 12 2003]. Available from http://www.taiaiake.com/home/index.html.

———. *Peace, Power, and Righteousness: an Indigenous manifesto*. Don Mills: Oxford University Press, 1999.

———. Personal communication, November 15 2002.

Alinsky, Saul. *Rules for Radicals: A Pragmatic Primer for Realistic Radicals*. New York: Vintage, 1971.

Alvesson, Mats and Skoldberg, Kaj. *Reflexive Methodology: New Vistas for Qualitative Research.* London: Sage Publications, 2000.

anonymous. Personal communication, August 5 2002.

Assefa, Hizkias. "The Meaning of Reconciliation." In *People Building Peace: 35 Inspiring Stories from around the World,* edited by European Centre for Conflict Prevention, 37-45. Utrecht: European Centre for Conflict Prevention, 1999.

———. "Peace and Reconciliation as a Paradigm: A Philosophy of Peace and Its Implications on Conflict, Governance and Economic Growth," 50. Nairobi, 2001.

———. "Philosophy and Praxis of Reconciliation." Paper presented at the Eastern Mennonite University Summer Peace-building Institute, Harrisonburg, May 16-24 2002.

Augsburger, David. *Conflict Mediation across Cultures: Pathways and Patterns.* Westminster: John Knox Press, 1992.

Banning Eyre/World Music Productions. *What Is a Griot?* 1997 [cited August 15 2003]. Available from http://artsedge.kennedy-center.org/aoi/html/griot.html.

Barkan, Elzar. *The Guilt of Nations: Restitution and Negotiating Historical Injustices.* Baltimore: The John Hopkins University Press, 2000.

Battiste, Marie, ed. *Reclaiming Indigenous Voice and Vision.* Vancouver: UBC Press, 2000.

Bavelas, Janet. "Apologies, Responsibility, and Restorative Justice: The Role of Language." Paper presented at the Centre for Studies in Religion and Society, University of Victoria, November 21 2001.

Baylands Productions. "The Unfolding Story." Palo Alto, 1993.

Bennett, Milton. "Towards Ethnorelativism: A Developmental Model of Intercultural Sensitivity." In *Education for the Intercultural Experience,* edited by Michael Paige, 1-51. Yarmouth: Intercultural Press, 1993.

Berry, Tomas. *The Great Work: Our Way into the Future.* New York: Bell Tower, 1999.

Bond, John. "A Strategy for a Real Australia." *Australian Newsbriefs,* October 2003.

Borris, Eileen. "The Healing Power of Forgiveness." *Institute for Multi-Track Diplomacy, occassional paper #10* 2003, 25.

Boulding, Elise; Brigagao, Clovis; Clements, Kevin. "Practice Love and Sustain Hope." In *A Handbook of International Peacebuilding: Into the Eye of the Storm*, edited by Lederach, John Paul and Jenner, Janice, 299-304. San Francisco: Jossey - Bass, 2002.

Bush, Robert and Folger, Joseph. *The Promise of Mediation*. San Francisco: Jossey Bass, 1994.

Campbell, Joseph. *Creative Mythology: The Masks of God*. New York: Penguin Books, 1968.

Capra, Fritjoff. *The Turning Point*. New York: Simon and Schuster, 1982.

Chrisjohn, et al. *The Circle Game: Shadows and Substance in Indian Residential School Experience in Canada*. Penticton: Theylus Books ltd., 1997.

Christian, Dorothy. Personal communication December 10 2003.

———. Email communication, January 15 2004.

———. "Living the Prophesy." In *Insight*, Vancouver: Vision TV, 2001/2002.

———. "One Small Step." Vancouver, 1999/2000 season.

———. "Witness." Vancouver: Vision Skylight, 1998.

Clark, Mary. *In Search of Human Nature*. New York: Routledge, 2002.

———. "Symptoms of Cultural Pathologies: A Hypothesis." In *Conflict Resolution Theory and Practice: Integration and Application*, edited by Dennis & van der Merwe Sandole, Hugo, 43-54. Manchester and New York: Manchester University Press, 1993.

Cohen, Stanley. *States of Denial: Knowing About Atrocities and Suffering*. Oxford: Blackwell Publishers, 2001.

The Commission On Children At Risk. *Hardwired to Connect: The New Scientific Case for Authoritative Communities* 2003 [cited November 15 2003]. Available from http://americanvalues.org/html/hardwired.html.

Cooper, Ardyth. Personal communication, September 15 2003.

Coulter, Philip. "The End of the Wild." In *CBC Ideas*. Toronto: CBC Ideas, 2001.

Crey, Ernie. "The Children of Tommorrow's Great Potlatch." *BC Studies Journal* 89 (1991): 150-58.

Cunneen, Chris. "Reparations and Restorative Justice: Responding to the Gross Violations of Human Rights." In *Restorative Justice and Civil Society*, edited by Heather Strang and John Braithwaite. Cambridge: Cambridge University Press, 2001.

Dasberg, Haim. *Myths and Taboos among Israeli First- and Second-Generation Psychiatrists in Regard to the Holocaust* 2000 [cited December 14 2003]. Available from http://www.holocaustechoes.com/dasberg2.html.

de Young, Mary. *Collective Trauma: Insights from a Research Errand* 1998 [cited October 20 2003]. Available from http://www.aaets.org/arts/art55.htm.

Demers, Maryse. "Lend Me Your Shoes." *Cantilevers* 6 (1999): 53.

Denis, Claude. *We Are Not You: First Nations and Canadian Modernity*. Peterborough: Broadview press, 1997.

deVries, M. "Trauma in Cultural Perspective." In *Traumatic Stress*, edited by A.C. McFarlane B.A. van der Kolk, & L. Weisaeth, 398-413. New York: The Guilford Press, 1996.

Docherty, Jayne. *Learning Lessons from Waco: When the Parties Bring Their Gods to the Negotiation Table*. Syracuse: Syracuse University Press, 2001.

Doe, Sam Gbaydee and Bombande, Emmanuel Habuka. "A View from West Africa." In *A Handbook of International Peacebuilding*, edited by Lederach, John Paul and Jenner, Janice, 159-70. San Francisco: Jossey-Bass, 2002.

Dunn, Larry. "The Process of Forgiveness-an Excercise." *MCS Conciliation Quarterly* (1995): 30-33.

Early Warning Risk Assessment [cited November 15 2003]. Available from www.fewer.org.

Eisenbruch, M. "From Post-Traumatic Stress Disorder to Cultural Bereavement: Diagnosis of Southeast Asian Refugees." *Social Science and Medicine* 33 (1991): 673-80.

Eliade, Mircea. *Birth and Rebirth: The Religious Meanings of Initiation in Human Culture*. New York: Harper & Brothers Publishers, 1958.

Erasmus, George. *Third Annual Lafontaine-Baldwin Lecture* 2002 [cited March 16 2002]. Available from http://cbc.ca/news/indepth/lafontaine_lectures/.

Eschatology Today, Sr Editor Mark Norris. *Hunting for Key Words the Inductive Way* 2004 [cited January 22 2004]. Available from www.eschatologytoday.net/keywordshtm.

Esteva, G. "Enough, Basta." *The Ecologist* 24, no. 3 (1994): 84.

Feehan, Margaret. "Stories of Healing from Native Indian Residential School Abuse." University of Victoria, 1996.

Fisher, Roger, William Ury and Bruce Patton. *Getting to Yes: Negotiating Agreement without Giving In.* 2nd ed. New York: Penguin Books, 1991.

Fitmaurice, Redmond. "Other Religions and Reconciliation," in *Reconciliation in Religion and Society*, edited by Michael Hurley. Belfast: Queens University of Belfast, 1994.

Gardner, Lois. Personal communication, July 15 2003.

Global Action to Prevent War. [cited November 15 2003]. Available from www.globalactionpw.org.

Green, Edward and Honwana, Alcinda. *Indigenous Healing of War Affected Children in Africa* No. 10, July 1999 [cited July 10, 2003]. Available from http://www.africaaction.org/docs99/viol9907.htm.

Grof, Christina and Grof, Stanislav. *The Stormy Search for Self.* New York: Jeremy P. Tarcher/Putnam, 1990.

Hahn, Thich Nhat. "Ahimsa: The Path of Harmlessness." In *Buddhist Peacework*, edited by David Chappell, 251. Boston: Wisdom Publications, 1999.

Hale, Charles. *Resistance and Contradiction: Miskitu Indians and the Nicuarguan State, 1894-1987.* Stanford: Stanford University Press, 1994.

Hanen, Bishop. Personal communication, October 31 2003.

Harper, Gary. Personal communication, July 7 2003.

———. "The Joy of Conflict Resolution: Transforming Victims, Villains and Heroes in the Workplace and at Home." Gabriola Island: New Society Publishers, 2004.

Harris, Cole. *Making Native Space: Colonialism, Resistance, and Reserves in British Columbia.* Vancouver and Toronto: University of British Columbia Press, 2002.

Hart, Barry. "Transforming Conflict through Trauma Recovery Training." Paper presented at the Trauma Recovery Training: Lessons Learned, Zagreb, Croatia, July 13-15 1997.

Hayner, Priscilla. *Unspeakable Truths: Confronting State Terror and Atrocity.* New York: Routledge, 2001.

Heelan, P.A. *Space, Perception and the Philosophy of Sciences.* Berkely: University of California Press, 1983.

Herman, Judith. *Trauma and Recovery: The Aftermath of Violence-from Domestic Abuse to Political Terror.* New York: Basic Books, 1997.

Hodgson, Maggie. "Residential School: 'A Shared Journey' in Redefining Relationships," 55. Edmonton, 2003.

Hoffman, Ben. "Eliminating Organized Violence." Metford, 2003.

hooks, bell. *All About Love: New Visions.* New York: William Morrow and Company, Inc., 2000.

Horse, Chief Arvol Looking. *A Call to Action* 2001 [cited December 15 2003]. Available from http://www.cleannorth.org/article/312.html?mode=nocomment.

Hyde, Lewis. *Trickster Makes This World.* New York: North Point Press, 1998.

Irani, George. "Rituals of Reconciliation: Arab-Islamic Perspectives." Paper presented at the Centre for Religion and Society Lecture Series, University of Victoria, March 13 2002.

James, Matt. "Redress Politics and Canadian Citizenship." In *Canada: The State of the Federation 1998/99: Exploring the Ties That Bind,* edited by Harvey and McIntosh Lazar, Tom, 247-81. Montreal and Kingston: McGill-Queen's University Press, 1999.

Johnstone, Gerry. *Restorative Justice: Ideas, Values, Debates.* Cullompton: Willan Publishing, 2002.

Joseph, Chief Robert. Personal communication, August 5 2003.

Jung, Carl. *Memories, Dreams, Reflections.* New York: Vintage Books, 1965.

Justice, International Centre for Transitional. 2003 [cited December 10 2003]. Available from http://www.ictj.org.

Keashly, Loraleigh and Warters, William. "Working It Out: Conflict in Interpersonal Contexts." In *Patterns of Conflict Paths to Peace,* edited by Larry & Schellenberg Fisk. Peterborough: Broadview Press, 2000.

Lahav, Hadas. "Against the Current, Women in Black." Paper presented at the Femme et Democratie au Moyen Orient, Concordia University, September 25 1993.

Lather, Patty. "Research as Praxis." *Harvard Educational Review* 56, no. 3 (1986): 257-77.

Lazare, Aaron. "The Healing Power of Apology." Paper presented at the Agenda For Reconciliation, Caux, Switzerland, August 6 2002.

LeBaron, Michelle. *Bridging Cultural Conflicts: A New Approach for a Changing World*. San Francisco: Jossey Bass, 2003.

———. *Bridging Troubled Waters: Conflict Resolution from the Heart*. San Francisco: Jossey-Bass, 2002.

Lederach, John Paul. *Building Peace: Sustainable Reconciliation in Divided Societies*. Washington D.C: United States Institute of Peace Press, 1997.

———. "Frontier Luncheon." Paper presented at the Eastern Mennonite University Summer Peace-building Institute, Harrisonburg, May 22 2002.

———. "Fundamentals of Peace-Building." Paper presented at the Eastern Mennonite University Conflict Transformation Program, Harrisonburg, January 6-10 2003.

———. *The Journey Toward Reconciliation*. Waterloo: Herald Press, 1999.

———. *Preparing for Peace: Conflict Transformation across Cultures*. Syracuse: Syracuse University Press, 1995.

Linn, Dennis; Linn, Sheila; and Linn, Mathew. *Don't Forgive Too Soon, Extending the Two Hands That Heal*. New York: Paulist Press, 1997.

Little Bear, Leroy. "Jagged Worldviews Colliding." In *Reclaiming Indigenous Voice and Vision*, edited by Marie Battiste. Vancouver: UBC Press, 2000.

Long, Anthony; Little Bear, Leroy; and Boldt, Menno. "Federal Policy and Indian Self-Government in Canada." In *Pathways to Self-Determination: Canadian Indians and the Canadian State*, edited by Little Bear, Leroy; Long, Anthony; and Boldt, Menno, 197. Toronto, Buffalo, and London: University of Toronto Press, 1992.

MacDonald, Kelly. "Literature Review: Implications of Restorative Justice in Cases of Violence against Aboriginal Women and Children." Vancouver: Aboriginal Women's Action Network, 2001.

MacGillis, Miriam Therese. "Exploring a New Cosmology: Reflections on the Writings of Thomas Berry and Brian Swimme." Pescadero, 2000.

Macy, Joanne. *Coming Back to Life: Practices to Reconnect Our Lives, Our World*. Gabriola Island: New Society Publishers, 1998.

———. *Widening Circles, a Memoir*. Gabriola Island: New Society Publishers, 2000.

Marcos, Subcommandante. *Our Word Is Our Weapon*. New York: Seven Stories Press, 2001.

Marshall, Joseph. *The Lakota Way: Stories and Wisdom for Living*. New York: Penguin Books, 2001.

Montville, Joseph. "Justice and the Burden of History." In *Reconciliation, Justice, and Coexistence: Theory and Practice*, edited by Mohammed Abu-Nimer, 129-43. Lanham: Lexington Books, 2001.

Morris, Catherine. *Interests, Needs, Rights, Morality and Conflict Resolution* 2003 [cited November 15 2003]. Available from http://www.peacemakers.ca/leadership/Morrisbib.html#papers.

Nahdi, Fuad. "Collapse of Civilizations." *For A Change* 16, no. 5 (2003): 24.

narrated by Farrell, Mike. "The Unfolding Story." 1993.

Nguyen, Anne. "Poetry, Politics, and Government from Plato to the Present." 21. Victoria, 2001.

Nicholls, William. "Working Together Respecting Differences." *Nation* 3, no. 22 (1996): 10-12 &22.

Nudler, Oscar. "On Conflicts and Metaphors." In *Conflict Human Needs Theory*, edited by John Burton. London: MacMillan Press, 1990.

O'Driscoll, Herbert. "The Raven and the Dove." Paper presented at the The Greater Victoria Lay School of Theology, Christ Church Cathedral, November 25 2003.

Panikkar, Raimon. "Is the Notion of Human Rights a Western Concept?" *Inter Culture*, no. 143 (2002): 42-60.

Parry, Danaan. *Warriors of the Heart*. Bainbridge Island: The Earthstewards Network, 1991.

Redekop, Vern. *From Violence to Blessing: How an Understanding of Deep-Rooted Conflict Can Open Paths to Reconciliation*. Ottawa: Novalis, 2002.

Ross, Rupert. *Returning to the Teachings: Exploring Aboriginal Justice*. Toronto: Penguin Books, 1996.

Ruremeshna, Jean. *Rwanda: Seeks to Close Overpopulated Prisons by Year-End* Inter Press Service, April 23 2003 [cited December 14 2003]. Available from http://www.afrika.no/Detailed/3398.html.

Sampson, Cynthia. "Positive Approaches to Peace-building." *MCS Conciliation Quarterly* 21, no. 1 (2002): 1-5.

Santos, Bonaventura De Sousa. *Toward a New Legal Common Sense: Law, Globalization, and Emancipation*. London: Butterworths Lexis Nexis, 2002.

Schechner, Richard and Appel, Willa, ed. *By Means of Performance: Intercultural Studies of Theatre and Ritual*. Cambridge: Cambridge University Press, 1990.

Schreiter, Robert. *Reconciliation: Mission & Ministry in a Changing Social Order*. New York: Orbis Books, 2002.

Service, Robert. [cited December 10 2003]. Available from www.cyber-nation.com/victory/quotations/authors/quotes-service_robertw.html.

Sharoni, Simona. "Israel: Is Feminism a Threat to National Security?"" *Ms* (1992).

Sovreignty, International Commission On Intervention and State. "The Responsibility to Protect: Report of the International Commission on Intervention on State Sovreignty." 91. Ottawa: International Development Research Centre, 2001.

Stewart, Wendy; Huntley, Audrey ; and Blaney, Fay. "The Implications of Restorative Justice for Aboriginal Women and Children Survivors of Violence: A Comparative Overview of Five Communities in British Columbia." Vancouver: Aboriginal Women's Action Network, 2001.

Stovel, Laura. "Unpublished Paper Reconciliation and Restorative Justice after Mass Atrocity: Clarifying Key Concepts." rough draft chapter in phD thesis, Simon Fraser University, 2002.

———. "Unpublished Paper Resotorative Justice in Post-War Contexts." Simon Fraser University, 2002.

Stubington, Cathy. Personal communication, December 15 2003.

———. "A Panel Discussion on Cultural Development." Paper presented at the Creative Cities Network Inaugural Conference, Morris J.Wosk Centre for Dialogue, Vancouver, November 2003.

Suman, Michael. *Religion and Prime Time Television*. Connecticut and London: Praeger Publishers, 1997.

Sutherland, Jessie. *Colonialism, Crime, and Dispute Resolution: A Critical Analysis of Canada's Aboriginal Justice Strategy* 2002 [cited December 10 2003]. Available from http://work.acresolution.org/research.nsf/key/Boskey-GradWinner2002.

Tarnas, Richard. *The Passion of the Western Mind: Understanding the Ideas That Have Shaped Our World View*. New York: Harmony Books, 1991.

Tidwell, Alan C. *Conflict Resolved? A Critical Assessment of Conflict Resolution*. London: Continuum, 1998.

Todd, Loretta. "Kainayssini Imanistaisiwa: The People Go On." edited by Loretta Todd. Toronto: National Film Board, 2003.

Toynbee, Arnold. *A Study of History*. 10 vols. London: Oxford University Press, 1955.

Tully, James. "Reconsidering the B.C. Treaty Process." Paper presented at the Speaking Truth To Power: A Treaty Forum, Ottawa, December 1 2003.

Tutu, Desmond. *No Future without Forgiveness*. New York: Doubleday, 1997.

Vachon, Robert. "Beyond the Religion of Human Rights, the Nation State, and the Rule of Law." *Inter Culture*, no. 143 (2002): 1-60.

———. "Guswenta or the Intercultural Imperative (a Sequel to Part I, Sections I and Ii) Section Iii: A New Method." *Inter Culture* XXVIII, no. 4 (1995): 2.

———. "Guswenta or the Intercultural Imperative (Continued) (Part I, Section Ii: A Common Horizon)." *Inter Culture* XXVIII, no. 3 (1995): 2-80.

———. "Guswenta or the Intercultural Imperative: Towards a Re-Enacted Peace Accord between the Mohawk Nation and the North American Nation-States (and Their People)." *Inter Culture* XXVIII, no. 127 (1995): 73.

Volkan, Vamik. *Blood Lines: From Ethnic Pride to Ethnic Terrorism*. Boulder: Westview Press, 1997.

Welsh, Paul. *Profile: Liberia's Rebels* 2003 [cited November 18 2003]. Available from http://news.bbc.co.uk/2/hi/africa/2979586.stm.

West African Network for Education and Peace. *Crisis in Cote D'ivoire* Fewer, 2003 [cited January 5 2004]. Available from www.fewer.org.

Wheatley, Margaret. *Turning to One Another: Simple Conversations to Restore Hope to the Future, Turning to One Another*. San Franscisco: Berrett Koehler Publishers, 2002.

Williamson, Marianne. *Healing the Soul of America: Reclaiming Our Voices as Spiritual Citizens*. New York: Touchstone, 1997.

Wilson, Richard A. *The Politics of Truth and Reconciliation in South Africa: Legitimizing the Post-Apartheid State.* Cambridge: Cambridge University Press, 2001.

Wink, Walter. *When the Powers Fall: Reconciliation in the Healing of Nations.* Minneapolis: Fortress Press: Minneapolis, 1998.

Winslade, John and Monk, Gerald. "Finding Common Ground between Traditional Adversaries: A Narrative Approach in Mediation." Paper presented at the American Anthropology Conference, New Orleans, November 2002.

Zehr, Howard. *The Little Book of Restorative Justice.* Intercourse: Good Books, 2002.

Worldview Strategies Workshops

Worldview Strategies offers a series of workshops for groups and organizations interested in learning skills for transforming relationships. This workshop series is ideal for week-long training intensives.

False and Genuine Reconciliation
In this introductory workshop, participants will learn about reconciliation in the global context, indicators for false reconciliation, and the elements that create conditions for genuine reconciliation. Through interactive activities, participants will explore reconciliation in their own lives and gain hands-on skills they can apply in their own context.

Meaning and Purpose
Some people die for a cause while others die because they have no cause. The global loss of meaning has lead to violence against others and self. In this workshop participants will explore how to deepen meaning and purpose in their own lives.

Conflict
In this workshop, participants will learn skills for engaging across worldview difference. This includes how to use intractable conflicts for personal awareness and growth and how to take care of our inherent fight and flight tendencies when we encounter conflict.

Who am I? Who are you?
Many people yearn for a deeper understanding of themselves and their relationships. In this workshop, participants will learn how to listen and watch in new ways that will lead to deeper insights into themselves and others.

Rituals
In this workshop, participants will learn key elements for creating transformative rituals in their own lives as well as have an opportunity to develop individual and group rituals.

If you would like more information about other Worldview Strategies services or would like to receive our free Monthly e-newsletter about *Tips and Strategies That Work*,
email: jessie@worldviewstrategies.com / call: 1-888-828-8180
visit: http://www.worldviewstrategies.com